Contents

06 What is PSYCHOLOGY?

08 What do PSYCHOLOGISTS DO?

10 Research METHODS

What makes me TICK?

14 Who needs PARENTS, anyway?

16 Can't you just GROW UP?

18 Can you be MOLDED?

20 You don't need no EDUCATION

22 Biography: IVAN PAVLOV

24 Live and LEARN

26 Why did you BEHAVE like that?

28 Do you know what's RIGHT AND WRONG?

30 Biography: MARY AINSWORTH

32 Is it never too LATE?

34 Developmental psychology in the REAL WORLD

What does my BRAIN do?

38 Is your MIND different from your BRAIN?

40 What goes on in your BRAIN?

42 What can BRAIN DAMAGE tell us?

44 Biography: SANTIAGO RAMÓN Y CAJAL

46 What is CONSCIOUSNESS?

48 Biography: VILANAYUR RAMACHANDRAN

50 DREAM on…

52 Biological psychology in the REAL WORLD

How does my MIND work?

56 What is KNOWLEDGE?

58 Decisions, decisions, DECISIONS

60 Why do you REMEMBER stuff?

62 Biography: ELIZABETH LOFTUS

64 How are memories STORED?

66 Don't TRUST your memory

68 Information OVERLOAD?

70 Biography: DONALD BROADBENT

72 Watch your LANGUAGE!

74 Are you FOOLING yourself?

76 How do you make SENSE of the world?

78 Don't BELIEVE your EYES

80 Cognitive psychology in the REAL WORLD

What makes me UNIQUE?

84 What makes you so SPECIAL?

86 What are you LIKE?

88 Biography: GORDON ALLPORT

90 So you think you're SMART?

92 Why are you so MOODY?

94 What MOTIVATES you?

96 Do PERSONALITIES change?

98 Feeling DOWN?

100 What makes an ADDICT?

102 Biography: SIGMUND FREUD

104 What is NORMAL?

106 Are you INSANE?

108 Is anyone really EVIL?

110 It's good to TALK

112 Is therapy the ANSWER?

114 Don't worry, be HAPPY!

116 Psychology of difference in the REAL WORLD

Where do I FIT IN?

120 Would you follow the CROWD?

122 Why do GOOD people do BAD things?

124 Don't be so SELFISH!

126 Biography: SOLOMON ASCH

128 ATTITUDE problem?

130 The power of PERSUASION

132 What makes you ANGRY?

134 Biography: STANLEY MILGRAM

136 Are you in the IN CROWD?

138 What makes a WINNING team?

140 Can you PERFORM under PRESSURE?

142 Do GUYS think like GIRLS?

144 Why do people fall in LOVE?

146 Social psychology in the REAL WORLD

148 Directory of psychologists

152 Glossary

156 Index and acknowledgments

What is **PSYCHOLOGY?**

PEOPLE ARE ENDLESSLY FASCINATING. THE CLOSER YOU LOOK, THE MORE
COMPLICATED THEY BECOME. PSYCHOLOGY IS A SCIENTIFIC DISCIPLINE THAT
IS DEVOTED TO UNDERSTANDING WHAT MAKES US WHO WE ARE. BY STUDYING
OUR MINDS AND OUR BEHAVIOR, IT SEEKS TO UNRAVEL THE IMMENSE, RICH
COMPLEXITY OF BEING HUMAN.

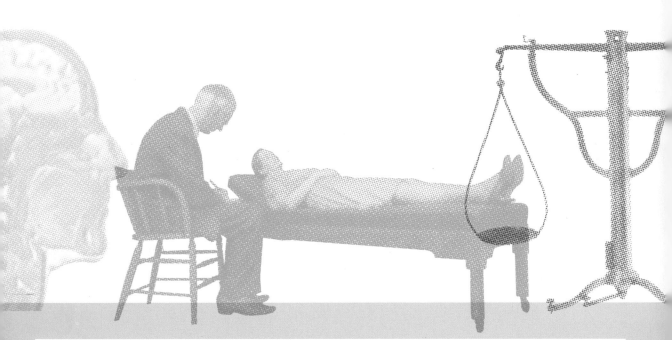

Think of the last time you took a bus or a train. Did you notice anyone else there? Did you strike up
a conversation with a fellow passenger? If so, is that because you are naturally outgoing, or was
there something particular to that situation that made you speak? You may have wondered why
you behave as you do. It is this curiosity about how people behave that drives psychologists, and
they ask such questions all the time. Psychology is the study of human behavior and the mind.
But what is the mind? It appears in our everyday speech: *I don't mind, I've changed my mind.*
The mind is not a physical thing, however, and it is not the same as the brain. It is a conceptual
mechanism with a set of abilities or functions. It doesn't matter that we cannot see it, nor can
we take it apart to see how it works. Psychologists try to imagine a way that it could possibly work,

and watch people to see if their behavior is consistent with that way of working. But people are difficult to study. The more you try to observe them, the more they change their behavior. Even so, huge advances have been made in our understanding of things such as how we form memories, make mistakes, interpret what we see, and communicate with other people. This has allowed us, in turn, to become better teachers, create a fairer justice system, build safer machines, treat mental disorders, and make many other advances. The journey toward understanding mind and behavior has taken about 140 years so far, but really we are just starting out. Every day, psychologists uncover new and surprising aspects of human behavior, but there is a long way to go before we can say that we truly understand the mind.

What do PSYCHOLOGISTS DO?

ACADEMIC PSYCHOLOGISTS

Social psychologists are interested in how people behave when they are together. They study human interaction, communication, attitudes, friendship, love, and conflict.

Social psychologist

By conducting carefully designed experiments, cognitive psychologists seek to define the mechanisms—such as memory—that make up our mind and allow us to behave as we do.

Cognitive psychologist

Also known as neuro- or biopsychologists, biological psychologists use scanners and other high-tech equipment to study the brain and learn about the biological basis of behavior.

Biological psychologist

MEDICAL PSYCHOLOGISTS

Often based in hospitals, clinical psychologists use a variety of therapies to help people cope with mental disorders such as depression or schizophrenia.

Clinical psychologist

Using therapy, clinical neuropsychologists can help people who have suffered from brain disease or injury regain the abilities they lost as a result of this brain damage.

Clinical neuropsychologist

APPLIED PSYCHOLOGISTS

How can a company get the most out of its workers? Organizational psychologists work in the business world and help make people more efficient and happier at their jobs.

Organizational psychologist

Using psychological research techniques, user experience (UX) researchers and designers create websites and programs that are indispensable, engaging, and intuitive.

User experience researcher/designer

THE ACTIVITIES OF PSYCHOLOGISTS ARE VERY DIVERSE, AND ACADEMIC PSYCHOLOGISTS REPRESENT ONLY A SMALL PROPORTION OF PEOPLE WITH PSYCHOLOGY QUALIFICATIONS. PSYCHOLOGY CAN BE USEFUL IN ALL KINDS OF AREAS WHERE THE QUALITY OF HUMAN BEHAVIOR IS CRITICAL, INCLUDING SPORTS, EDUCATION, HEALTH, AND AVIATION. IN ADDITION, MANY OF THE SKILLS PSYCHOLOGISTS LEARN ARE USEFUL IN OTHER CAREERS.

Studying how our minds have evolved over time allows evolutionary psychologists to understand where abilities such as reasoning and language may have come from.

Evolutionary psychologist

How do we change from helpless infants into adults with many abilities? The study of development allows psychologists to see how we build our minds as we grow.

Developmental psychologist

These psychologists are interested in finding the best ways to teach people. They test different theories of education, and come up with ways of improving teaching styles.

Educational psychologist

Individual differences psychologists look at what makes each person unique. This includes ideas about personality, emotions, intelligence, identity, and mental health.

Individual differences psychologist

Using specific counseling methods, these psychologists help people cope with and overcome challenges in their lives, such as bereavement or relationship issues.

Counseling psychologist

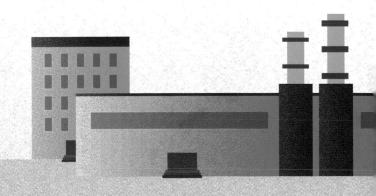

Most commonly working in the transportation industry, human factors specialists improve the design of signs, controls, and interfaces to improve safety on the roads and in the air.

Human factors specialist

Many psychologists work in human resources, where they manage employees, helping them with their career progression, appraisals, and any difficulties they may encounter.

Human resources

Research **METHODS**

THIS BOOK CONTAINS AN OVERVIEW OF SOME OF THE MOST IMPORTANT FINDINGS IN PSYCHOLOGY. BUT HOW DID PSYCHOLOGISTS FIRST ARRIVE AT THEIR RESULTS AND THEORIES? RESEARCH METHODS IN PSYCHOLOGY HAVE BECOME MORE AND MORE COMPLEX OVER THE YEARS, BUT THE BASIC APPROACH REMAINS THE SAME. USING THE CORRECT METHODS ALLOWS PSYCHOLOGISTS TO CONDUCT ACCURATE AND RELIABLE RESEARCH, FORMING A SOLID BASIS FOR THEIR THEORIES.

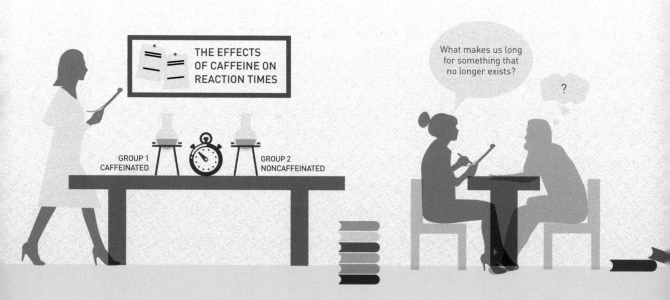

Laboratory conditions

Psychologists perform experiments in the laboratory, where they create two or more controlled conditions and try to measure the difference in behavior between people in those conditions. For example, one group of people might be given a caffeinated drink, while another receives a noncaffeinated drink, to test whether or not caffeine affects reaction times. This allows researchers to conclude that the different conditions caused any variations in behavior.

Deep and meaningful

Psychologists are interested in the meaning behind people's behavior, and use qualitative techniques to explore topics when their observations are not easily converted into numbers. For example, to investigate the nature of nostalgia, a psychologist might use interviews and open-ended questionnaires to find out more about people's experiences of the sensation. The psychologist can then interpret this subjective material to draw conclusions about human behavior.

Statistical analysis

Some of the most powerful evidence in psychology comes from quantitative (numerical) methods. Psychologists design a variety of tests to measure and compare people's personalities, for example, and predict how they will behave in the future. This data can be used to construct graphs—to show how personality varies by location, for instance. The advantage of using this approach lies in its ability to reveal patterns that may be too subtle to see otherwise.

Out in the real world

Sometimes, it's impossible to obtain meaningful results from a controlled experiment or by using qualitative techniques such as interviews. In cases where the behavior in question is dependent on the environment or situation—for example, public transportation—psychologists enter the situation and try to analyze behavior systematically. However, researchers have to be extremely careful not to interfere with that behavior, or they risk jeopardizing their results.

What makes me TICK?

Who needs PARENTS, anyway?

Can't you just GROW UP?

Can you be MOLDED?

You don't need no EDUCATION

Live and LEARN

Why did you BEHAVE like that?

Do you know what's RIGHT AND WRONG?

Is it never too LATE?

Developmental psychology looks at the way we change throughout our lives, and the stages we go through, from birth to childhood to our turbulent teenage years to adulthood and eventually old age. It includes the study of how we acquire skills and knowledge, and learn about good and bad behavior.

See also: 30–31

Who needs

AS SMALL CHILDREN, WE NEED ADULTS TO CARE FOR US AND PROVIDE US WITH FOOD, WARMTH, AND SHELTER. THESE CAREGIVERS, USUALLY OUR PARENTS, ARE ALSO IMPORTANT TO OUR PSYCHOLOGICAL DEVELOPMENT. WE FORM EMOTIONAL BONDS WITH THEM FROM AN EARLY AGE, WHICH GIVES US THE SECURITY WE NEED TO EXPLORE AND LEARN ABOUT THE WORLD.

Forming crucial bonds

While studying the behavior of animals, early 20th-century biologist Konrad Lorenz noticed the strong bond between young geese and their mothers. He discovered that chicks form an attachment to the first moving thing they

separated from their parents for long periods of time, including child evacuees from World War II. He noticed that many of these children developed intellectual, social, or emotional problems later in life. Bowlby concluded that in the first 24 months of life, children have an essential need to develop a bond with at least one adult caregiver—usually a parent, and most often the mother. Attachment is different from other relationships in that it is a strong and lasting emotional tie with one particular person, which, if disturbed, can have long-term effects on development.

> MOTHER-**LOVE** IN INFANCY IS AS IMPORTANT FOR **MENTAL HEALTH** AS ARE VITAMINS AND PROTEINS FOR PHYSICAL HEALTH.
> **JOHN BOWLBY**

see after they hatch—this is usually their mother, but it could also be a "foster parent." Lorenz realized that chicks do not learn this behavior; it is an instinctive phenomenon, which he called "imprinting." Later, psychologists started to take an interest in the bond between newborn babies and their parents, which they called "attachment." One of the first to study attachment, John Bowlby, observed children who had been

SECURE
THESE CHILDEN ARE WILLING TO EXPLORE AND ENGAGE WITH STRANGERS IF THEIR MOTHERS ARE THERE, BUT ARE DISTRESSED WHEN THEY LEAVE AND HAPPY TO SEE THEM RETURN.

Stranger danger

Mary Ainsworth, who worked for a time with Bowlby in London, continued this research. She believed that the attachment figure (the caregiver to whom the infant attaches) provides a secure base from which the child can learn to explore the world. In her "Strange Situation" experiment, Ainsworth studied how infants reacted to a stranger, first with

THERE ARE THREE TYPES OF ATTACHMENT...

PARENTS, anyway?

> children with attachment disorders often act younger—both socially and emotionally.

their mothers in the room, and then without them. The results (shown here on the balloons) suggested that there are three different types of attachment: secure, anxious-resistant, and anxious-avoidant. A secure attachment creates a positive template for a child's future relationships. In contrast, evidence suggests that nonsecurely attached children find it more difficult to form strong relationships later in life.

ANXIOUS-AVOIDANT
THESE CHILDREN LARGELY IGNORE THEIR MOTHERS WHEN PLAYING, AND ALTHOUGH THEY'RE DISTRESSED WHEN LEFT ALONE, THEY CAN BE EASILY COMFORTED BY A STRANGER.

One big family

While Bowlby and Ainsworth stressed the importance of the mother-child relationship, some psychologists believe that an infant can bond with other people and still develop healthily. Michael Rutter showed that infants can form strong attachments to their fathers, siblings, friends, or even inanimate objects. Bruno Bettelheim also questioned the value of the specific mother-child bond. In a study of an Israeli *kibbutz*, where children were raised communally away from the family home, he found little evidence of emotional turmoil. In fact, the children often went on to have active social lives and good careers. But critics pointed out that they also tended to form fewer close relationships as adults.

ANXIOUS-RESISTANT
THESE CHILDREN AVOID STRANGERS AND ARE RELUCTANT TO EXPLORE. THEY ARE VERY DISTRESSED WHEN SEPARATED FROM THEIR MOTHERS, AND ARE ANGRY WITH THEM ON THEIR RETURN.

CUDDLY MONKEYS

Psychologist Harry Harlow introduced infant monkeys to artificial "mothers." Some were padded with cloth; others were left as bare wire, but provided food in a bottle. The monkeys fed from the bottle but soon went back to the cuddly "mother" for comfort. This highlighted the importance of meeting a child's emotional, as well as physical, needs.

6–12 YEARS
WE LEARN NEW SKILLS
AND FIND OUT WHAT WE'RE
GOOD AT, DEVELOPING
OUR SELF-CONFIDENCE.

12–18 YEARS
WE START TO WONDER ABOUT
THE PURPOSE OF LIFE AND
OUR PLACE IN SOCIETY,
DEVELOPING OUR SENSE
OF IDENTITY.

3–6 YEARS
WE PLAY MORE CREATIVELY,
BUT LEARN THAT WE CAN'T
DO WHATEVER WE WANT
BECAUSE OUR ACTIONS AFFECT
OTHER PEOPLE.

Can't you just GROW UP?

the adolescent brain is at a stage of development that makes teenagers take more risks than adults.

1–3 YEARS
WE START TO DEVELOP
INDEPENDENCE AND
WILLPOWER BY EXPLORING,
BUT WE ALSO LEARN TO
DEAL WITH FAILURE
AND DISAPPROVAL.

FOR MUCH OF HUMAN HISTORY, CHILDREN WERE SEEN AS SIMPLY "MINIATURE ADULTS" WHOSE MINDS WORKED IN THE SAME WAY, BUT WITHOUT THE SAME KNOWLEDGE. IT WAS NOT UNTIL THE 20TH CENTURY THAT PSYCHOLOGISTS REALIZED THAT, JUST AS OUR BODIES DEVELOP AS WE GROW OLDER, SO DO OUR MINDS.

Becoming civilized

A pioneer in the field of developmental psychology, G. Stanley Hall was the first to suggest that our minds develop in distinct stages: childhood, adolescence, and adulthood. After our initial growth as a child, he suggested, we go through a turbulent time in our teenage years, when we are self-conscious, sensitive, and reckless, before emerging as what he called a "civilized" adult. In the 1930s, Swiss psychologist Jean Piaget realized that the early years of childhood are critical. He described four stages of mental development, which all children pass through in the same sequence. According to his theory, children can only move on to the next stage after completing the current stage. Most crucially, Piaget stressed that they do this by exploring the world physically, rather than by instruction. By trying things out slowly for themselves, they build up knowledge and skills.

0–1 YEARS
WE LEARN TO TRUST OUR
PARENTS AND FEEL SAFE,
WHICH BECOMES THE
BASIS FOR OUR SENSE
OF IDENTITY.

See also: 24–25, 28–29, 32–33

AS WE AGE,
WE GO THROUGH
DIFFERENT STAGES OF
DEVELOPMENT...

18–35 YEARS
WE DEVELOP NEW INTIMATE RELATIONSHIPS AND FRIENDSHIPS, AND BUILD ON EXISTING ONES.

Exploring the world

In Piaget's first stage (0–2 years), children learn about things around them through their senses of sight, hearing, touch, taste, and smell, and they learn how to control the movements of their bodies. In this sensorimotor stage, they become aware of objects and other people, but see everything from their own viewpoint, and cannot understand that others have a different perspective. In stage two, the

ADMIRING YOURSELF

In a study designed to measure children's self-awareness, infants between the ages of 6 and 24 months were put in front of a mirror after someone had secretly put a dab of makeup on their noses. When asked "Who's that?" the younger children thought the reflection was another child, but the older children recognized themselves and pointed at the makeup on their noses. This study showed that we develop a sense of self-awareness around the age of 18 months.

> # A CHILD'S MIND IS FUNDAMENTALLY DIFFERENT FROM AN ADULT'S MIND.
> **JEAN PIAGET**

preoperational stage (2–7 years), children learn new skills, such as the ability to move and arrange objects—according to height or color, for example. They also become aware that other people have their own thoughts and feelings. In stage three, the concrete operational stage (7–11 years), children can perform more logical operations, but only with physical objects. For instance, they understand that if they pour a liquid from a short, wide glass into a tall, thin one, the amount of liquid stays the same. It is not until stage four, the formal operational stage (11 years onward), that children move beyond this and become capable of thinking about abstract ideas, such as love, fear, guilt, envy, and right and wrong.

Life's pros and cons

Piaget's notion of distinct stages of mental development in children was enormously influential in both psychology and education. Yet some psychologists thought that our development does not end when we become adults, but that we continue to evolve psychologically throughout our lives. In the 1950s, Erik Erikson identified eight definite stages of psychological development, from infancy to old age. He described this as a "ground plan," in which each stage is defined by a conflict between positive and negative aspects of our lives—at school or work, and in our relationships with family and friends. For example, at 3–6 years, we face a conflict between initiative and guilt: We start to do things the way we want, but we may end up feeling guilty if our actions affect others. At 18–35 years, we face intimacy or isolation: We may develop close relationships, but if these fail, we feel lonely. By the final stage, we should feel a sense of achievement, assuming we have experienced the positive aspects of earlier stages.

35–65 YEARS
WE SETTLE DOWN AND FEEL A SENSE OF ACHIEVEMENT, PERHAPS FROM RAISING CHILDREN OR PROGRESSING IN A CAREER.

65+ YEARS
WE FEEL A SENSE OF SATISFACTION AND ACCOMPLISHMENT FROM WHAT WE HAVE ACHIEVED IN LIFE.

Can you

WE LIKE TO THINK THAT WE'RE IN CONTROL OF WHAT WE DO AND THE CHOICES WE MAKE IN LIFE. BUT OUR BEHAVIOR IS, TO SOME EXTENT, SHAPED BY WHAT HAPPENS TO US AND OUR RESPONSE TO THOSE EXPERIENCES. SOME PSYCHOLOGISTS HAVE ARGUED THAT IT IS POSSIBLE TO MOLD PEOPLE'S BEHAVIOR, AND EVEN TRAIN THEM TO DO JUST ABOUT ANYTHING.

Stimulus and response

It was a Russian physiologist, not a psychologist, who made the first discoveries about how animals can be stimulated to respond in a certain way. Ivan Pavlov was carrying out experiments to measure the amount of saliva dogs secreted during eating, when he noticed that the dogs started salivating ahead of schedule, when they thought that food was on its way. Intrigued, Pavlov took his investigations further by giving a signal, such as a ringing bell, each time food was provided. He found that the dogs soon learned to associate the signal with food, and after a while their mouths watered every time they heard the bell—even when there was no food. Pavlov explained that the dogs had been "conditioned" to respond to the bell. When they salivated at the sight of food, this was a natural or "unconditioned" response, but when they salivated at the sound of the bell, this was a new, conditioned response. This pattern of stimulus and response became known as classical conditioning.

We are born as blank slates

A group of psychologists known as behaviorists built on Pavlov's theory of classical conditioning to explain why humans behave the way they do. John B. Watson believed that children are "blank slates"—they are born with no knowledge, and can be taught anything using classical conditioning. In his opinion, the human emotions of fear, rage, and love are the key to how we behave. He showed that we can be conditioned to give one

Career choice? ➔

John B. Watson believed that all babies are born knowing nothing, but that any child's path in life—including his or her future career— could be controlled through conditioning.

TEACHER

ANYONE CAN BE TRAINED TO DO ANYTHING.

SOCCER PLAYER

be **MOLDED**?

of these emotional responses in reaction to a stimulus, just as Pavlov's dogs were conditioned to give a physical reaction (see Little Albert, below). But Watson's use of conditioning on humans was very controversial, and later psychologists preferred not to try to condition human subjects, especially children.

Trial and error

Other behaviorist psychologists continued to experiment with animals, believing that what they learned about animal behavior could be applied to humans. Edward Thorndike devised a series of experiments that showed how cats learn to solve problems. A hungry cat was put into a "puzzle box," and had to figure out how to use a mechanism such as a button or lever to open the box, in order to escape and reach its food.

Thorndike observed that the cats found the mechanism by trial and error, and forgot any actions that

Following in Ivan Pavlov's footsteps, many dog trainers use classical conditioning to train their pets.

> **GIVE ME A DOZEN HEALTHY INFANTS... AND I'LL GUARANTEE TO TAKE ANY ONE OF THEM AT RANDOM AND TRAIN HIM TO BECOME ANY TYPE OF SPECIALIST.**
> JOHN B. WATSON

weren't successful. He concluded that animals, including humans, learn by making links between actions and results; he emphasized that success or reward reinforces these links, which are further strengthened by the repetition of the action. Edwin Guthrie also studied animals in puzzle boxes, and agreed that they learned to associate actions with rewards. Unlike Thorndike, however, Guthrie asserted that there was no need for any repetition of the action to reinforce the learning. He explained this using the example of a rat that has discovered a source of food: "Once a rat has visited our grain sack, we can plan on its return."

See also: 26–27, 28–29

LITTLE ALBERT

John B. Watson conducted several controversial experiments on a nine-month-old child, "Little Albert," making him associate the appearance of a white rat (and other white, furry things) with terrifying loud noises. Albert became conditioned to be afraid of anything white and furry. It is now considered unethical to experiment on human subjects in this way, since it can lead to long-term trauma.

DOCTOR

You don't need no EDUCATION

playing with colored blocks helps children learn about geometry and spatial awareness.

WE LEARN

TRADITIONALLY, LEARNING WAS SEEN AS SIMPLY A MATTER OF MEMORIZING INFORMATION. BUT AS PSYCHOLOGISTS EXAMINED THE WAY WE LEARN THINGS, IDEAS ABOUT EDUCATION CHANGED. THEY FOUND THAT LEARNING BY ROTE, OR REPETITION, IS NOT THE BEST METHOD— WE DO NEED TO STUDY, BUT HOW WE STUDY IS VERY IMPORTANT, TOO.

Making it stick

The way we learn things and how our memories work are of great interest to psychologists. Hermann Ebbinghaus, a 19th-century pioneer of psychology, studied memory and found that the longer and more often we spend time memorizing something, the better we remember it. This confirmed the idea that to learn something well, we should study hard and often. A century later, behaviorist psychologists suggested that we learn by experience, and that when we do something that is rewarded, we remember and can repeat it. Some of the behaviorists, including Edward Thorndike and

B. F. Skinner, also emphasized the importance of reinforcing that learning by repetition—going over what you have learned to make it stick. Unlike Ebbinghaus, however, Skinner stressed that there should be some kind of reward for every successful repetition. He invented a "teaching machine," which gave feedback to students in the form of praise for correct answers, but asked them to repeat questions that they answered incorrectly.

Understanding is the key to learning

But even Ebbinghaus realized there is much more to learning something thoroughly than simply repeating it. He found that we remember things much better if

THE ART OF RAISING CHALLENGING QUESTIONS IS EASILY AS IMPORTANT AS THE ART OF GIVING CLEAR ANSWERS.

JEROME BRUNER

EDUCATION

BEST THROUGH PRACTICAL EXPERIENCE.

↩ **Hands-on learning**

Children of different ages have different needs when it comes to education. Jean Piaget emphasized the importance of practical experience—doing an experiment, for example, or building a model.

PEEKABOO

According to Piaget, children can only learn things that fit their stage of development. In one study, Piaget showed a child a toy, which he then hid under a cloth while the child was watching. He found that children older than eight months knew to look for the toy under the cloth, but that infants younger than eight months could not understand that the toy was still there even though it was hidden from view.

See also: 16–17, 56–57, 58–59

they have some significance or meaning to us. Later psychologists returned to this idea. They approached it from the point of view of what is going on in our minds as we learn, rather than how things can be made to stick in our memories. Since Ebbinghaus showed that we remember things better if they mean something, psychologists came to believe that we learn by trying to make sense of things. Wolfgang Köhler suggested that, in trying to solve problems, we get an insight into the way things work. Edward Tolman went further, suggesting that we each build up a mental "map" of the world from the ideas we learn. Combining these ideas with his own notion of the mind as a processor of information, Jerome Bruner showed that learning is not simply a matter of putting information into our memories, but involves a process of thinking and reasoning. To learn something well, we have to understand it first.

Do it to learn it

Jean Piaget approached the idea of learning from yet another angle. He saw it in terms of the stages of mental development he had distinguished in children. Children's learning, he said, is a process that changes

THE GOAL OF EDUCATION IS TO CREATE MEN AND WOMEN WHO ARE CAPABLE OF DOING NEW THINGS.

JEAN PiAGET

to fit the limitations of each stage of development. He incorporated the behaviorist theory that chidren learn through trial and error, especially in the early stages, with the cognitive theory that we learn by making sense of what we discover. But, most importantly, he stressed that education should be child-centered— geared to children's individual needs and abilities, and encouraging children to use their imaginations in exploring and understanding the world for themselves. In the early stages, this would take the form of what we regard as "play" (which from a child's point of view is very serious). And as children get older, learning is most likely to succeed through hands-on experience, as opposed to learning by rote from a teacher or from books.

IVAN PAVLOV

1849–1936

Born in Ryazan, Russia, Ivan Pavlov originally studied to be a priest like his father, but left theological college and moved to Saint Petersburg to study science and medical surgery. He became a professor at the Military Medical Academy, and later director of the Institute of Experimental Medicine. Although he is best known for being a brilliant physiologist, his work laid the foundations of behaviorist psychology.

DOG'S DINNER

Pavlov is famous for his experiments on salivating dogs. He noticed that the dogs' mouths watered at the prospect of food—what he called an unconditioned response to an unconditioned stimulus. If he rang a bell each time food was presented to the dogs, they would start to salivate whenever a bell rang. This process of provoking a specific response with a specific stimulus became known as classical conditioning.

REVERSING RESPONSES

In later experiments, Pavlov showed that conditioning could be reversed. The dogs that had been conditioned to salivate when a bell rang, for example, could "unlearn" that response if no food was presented to them. He also showed that animals could be conditioned to respond with fear or anxiety if the stimulus was associated with a punishment, such as an electric shock, instead of a reward.

"The **sight of tasty food** makes a hungry man's **mouth water**."

STRICT CONDITIONS

Psychologists were influenced both by Pavlov's discoveries and by the methods he used. True to his training as a scientist, Pavlov conducted his experiments under strict scientific conditions. Psychology was just beginning to emerge as a separate discipline at the end of the 19th century, and, by adopting Pavlov's methodical approach, psychologists established the new science of experimental psychology.

Pavlov was nominated for a Nobel Prize in four consecutive years, and eventually won the Prize for Physiology or Medicine in 1904.

SPEAKING OUT

Pavlov was the director of the Institute of Experimental Medicine when the tsar was overthrown during the Russian Revolution and the Communist Soviet Union was established. Even though the government regarded him highly and continued to fund his work, Pavlov detested the Communist regime. He was quite open with his criticism, and wrote many letters to Soviet leaders to protest against the persecution of Russian intellectuals.

Live and LEARN

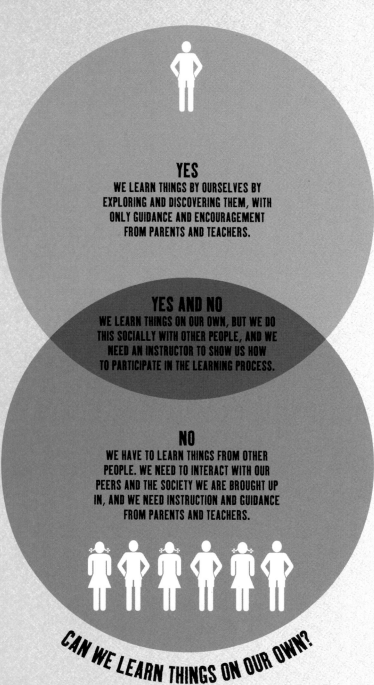

YES
WE LEARN THINGS BY OURSELVES BY EXPLORING AND DISCOVERING THEM, WITH ONLY GUIDANCE AND ENCOURAGEMENT FROM PARENTS AND TEACHERS.

YES AND NO
WE LEARN THINGS ON OUR OWN, BUT WE DO THIS SOCIALLY WITH OTHER PEOPLE, AND WE NEED AN INSTRUCTOR TO SHOW US HOW TO PARTICIPATE IN THE LEARNING PROCESS.

NO
WE HAVE TO LEARN THINGS FROM OTHER PEOPLE. WE NEED TO INTERACT WITH OUR PEERS AND THE SOCIETY WE ARE BROUGHT UP IN, AND WE NEED INSTRUCTION AND GUIDANCE FROM PARENTS AND TEACHERS.

CAN WE LEARN THINGS ON OUR OWN?

IN THE PAST, IT SEEMED OBVIOUS THAT PARENTS AND TEACHERS SIMPLY TAUGHT YOUNG PEOPLE INFORMATION AND SHOWED THEM HOW TO DO THINGS. BUT NEW IDEAS SUGGESTED THAT CHILDREN LEARN BY DISCOVERING THINGS FOR THEMSELVES. PSYCHOLOGISTS HAVE SINCE STARTED WONDERING HOW MUCH WE CAN LEARN ON OUR OWN, AND WHETHER OR NOT WE NEED TO BE TAUGHT BY OTHER PEOPLE.

Young scientists

Jean Piaget was one of the first to question the traditional roles of parents and teachers in educating children. In his view, adults should not try to dictate knowledge and skills, but should simply encourage children to learn things by themselves. Piaget believed that children need to explore and be creative on their own in order to learn about the world around them. At its heart, his theory was based on the notion that learning is a personal process—one that each child experiences on his or her own. A child, he thought, is like a scientist who conducts experiments to see how things work, and learns the principles by observing and understanding the results. These ideas were very influential and inspired the introduction of more child-centered education systems, in which children learn from practical activities, rather than passive observation.

spending time playing in green outdoor spaces may help children learn creative skills.

Young apprentices

Piaget's theories were quite revolutionary, and not all psychologists agreed with them. Lev Vygotsky, for example, stressed the importance of other people in a child's education. He believed that teachers should still take an instructive role, constantly guiding pupils on what and how to learn, rather than letting them find out for themselves. He rejected the image of children as scientists making discoveries on their own, and presented the alternative idea of children as apprentices, learning skills and knowledge from other people. Although we do make some discoveries for ourselves, he believed that learning is an interactive process. We absorb values and knowledge from our parents and teachers, and also from our wider culture. We then learn how to use that knowledge, along with the knowledge we've learned for ourselves, through experiences with our peers. In the late 20th century, the revival of Vygotsky's ideas led to a shift from child-centered to curriculum-centered teaching, in which lessons follow established guidelines.

A bit of both

Piaget and Vygotsky presented two apparently opposite theories. But both describe learning as a process in which children are actively involved—an idea that appealed to the cognitive psychologist

> # TO INSTRUCT SOMEONE... IS TO TEACH HIM TO PARTICIPATE IN THE PROCESS.
>
> **JEROME BRUNER**

After exercise, your body produces a chemical that helps your brain absorb information.

Jerome Bruner. He agreed with Piaget that we are not taught in the traditional sense, but that we acquire knowledge through exploration and discovery. And he agreed that learning is a process that each child must experience for his- or herself. But he also thought, like Vygotsky, that this is a social process, not a solitary occupation. In order to learn, we have to make sense of things through hands-on experience, and doing this with other people helps the process. For Bruner, the role of the instructor (a parent or teacher) is a vital one—not to tell or show children what they need to know, but to guide them through the learning experience. Today, most educators use a similar balance of formal teaching and hands-on learning.

See also: 16–17, 20–21

ARRANGING THE FURNITURE

Two groups of children were asked to put items of furniture into the different rooms of a dollhouse. In one group, each child was left to work alone, but in the other group the children performed the task with their mothers. When they were asked to repeat the task alone, the children from the second group showed more improvement on their first attempt than the "loners." This indicates that children learn best if they are encouraged by an adult.

> # WE BECOME OURSELVES THROUGH OTHERS.
>
> **LEV VYGOTSKY**

Why did you

AS WE GROW UP, WE LEARN NOT ONLY KNOWLEDGE AND SKILLS BUT ALSO HOW TO BEHAVE IN EVERYDAY LIFE. SOME PSYCHOLOGISTS BELIEVE THAT OUR BEHAVIOR IS SHAPED BY THE APPROVAL OR DISAPPROVAL OF OTHER PEOPLE, SUCH AS PARENTS AND TEACHERS, WHILE OTHERS THINK THAT WE SIMPLY IMITATE WHAT WE SEE OTHER PEOPLE DOING.

Rewarding behavior

The experiments of early behaviorist psychologists, such as John B. Watson and Edward Thorndike, showed that animals—including humans—can be conditioned to do things, and led to the belief that our behavior is the result of stimulus and response, or classical conditioning. B. F. Skinner, a later behaviorist, carried out similar studies using rats and pigeons, and showed that they could be trained not only to do things, but also *not* to do things. He used a type of conditioning called "operant conditioning." This involved giving the animals positive reinforcement (Skinner preferred this term to the word *reward*), in the form of food pellets, when they successfully completed a task, and negative reinforcement (punishment), in the form of electric shocks, when they

PEOPLE COPY OTHER PEOPLE'S BEHAVIOR—GOOD AND BAD.

Learning bad habits

Albert Bandura believed that we learn our behavior by copying others. If a child hears an adult use a swear word, for example, it is likely that the child will go on to repeat the offensive word.

BEHAVE like that?

> we pick up habits at home: **Most** children watch the same amount of television as their parents.

did something he wanted to train them not to do. Skinner believed operant conditioning could be used to shape children's behavior—for example, by praising their achievements—but he was uneasy about punishing undesirable behavior, preferring more positive reinforcement. Although the idea of operant conditioning explains how we can be taught to behave in a certain way, it doesn't necessarily teach us why that behavior is considered desirable or undesirable.

Setting an example

Other psychologists suggested that it is not just the way parents, teachers, and other caregivers reward or punish us that shapes our behavior. Albert Bandura believed that we learn our behavior by example. Seeing the way other people behave, we notice that there is a pattern to their actions in various situations. We then assume that these behaviors are normal for each situation—what are known as social and cultural "norms." We remember how people behave, and rehearse this behavior in our minds so that when we find ourselves in the same situation, we know how to react. This way of "modeling" behavior, by observing and then imitating other people, was the central idea in what Bandura called "social learning theory."

Picking up prejudice

Another aspect of social learning is that we pick up attitudes from other people. While that can be a good thing—teaching

> ## BEHAVIOR IS SHAPED BY POSITIVE AND NEGATIVE REINFORCEMENT.
>
> B. F. SKINNER

us about the beliefs that shape our culture, for example—it can also have a negative side. Social attitudes in many societies include prejudices such as racism. In 1940, husband-and-wife psychologists Kenneth and Mamie Clark studied the way that segregated African-American children and their white counterparts learned attitudes. Both groups of children were presented with a white doll and a black doll, and were asked which doll they preferred. Most children, black and white, chose the white doll, suggesting that they had absorbed from their communities the attitude that black people were inferior to white people—even though, for the black children, this prejudice was against themselves.

See also: 18–19, 28–29

DOLL BASHING

In one of Albert Bandura's experiments, some children watched adults behave aggressively toward a "Bobo doll." Another group was shown adults acting passively with the doll, and a control group was shown no adults with the doll. When left alone with the doll, the children who had witnessed aggression also acted violently toward the doll, but the others didn't. This confirmed Bandura's view that we learn behavior through copying other people.

Do you know what's

LEARNING THE DIFFERENCE BETWEEN GOOD AND BAD BEHAVIOR IS AN IMPORTANT PART OF GROWING UP. BEHAVIORISTS THOUGHT THAT GOOD AND BAD ACTIONS WERE CONDITIONED BY REWARDS AND PUNISHMENTS, BUT LATER PSYCHOLOGISTS SUGGESTED THAT WE ACQUIRE OUR SENSE OF RIGHT AND WRONG IN DISTINCT STAGES.

Alarmingly, studies have shown that 60 percent of people will lie at least once during a ten-minute conversation.

Moral teaching

For a long time, it was thought that children's moral development—learning about right and wrong—was determined by teaching. Behaviorist psychologists believed that moral behavior could be shaped by conditioning. Using the idea of stimulus and response, they thought that good behavior could be conditioned by rewards, and bad behavior discouraged by punishment. But others pointed out that most people haven't committed a serious crime and been punished for it, yet they know that murder, for example, is wrong. And although

IN THE SIMPLEST OF SOCIAL GAMES, WE FIND RULES WHICH HAVE BEEN ELABORATED BY THE CHILDREN ALONE.

JEAN PIAGET

psychologists such as Albert Bandura suggested that we learn by imitating others, children who play aggressive video games generally don't go on to act violently, since they know this is wrong.

The rules of the game

A large part of Jean Piaget's study of children's development focused on their moral development. He interviewed

MORALITY DEVELOPS IN SIX STAGES.

LAWRENCE KOHLBERG

children of different ages, asking what they thought about morally wrong things such as stealing and lying, and observed them playing games together. As with their psychological development in general, he found that children develop a sense of morality in stages. And, just as he thought that they learn best by exploring the world on their own, rather than through instruction from a teacher, he suggested that children develop their ideas of right and wrong, fair and unfair, themselves, through their relationships with others of the same age. In games, children make rules that reflect their evolving notions of justice, equality, and reciprocity (give and take)—quite independently of teachers, parents, or other authority figures.

Steps in the right direction

About 25 years after Piaget's theory of moral development, Lawrence Kohlberg took the ideas a step further. He agreed that we develop a sense of morality in gradual stages, but felt that authority figures and society in general do have an influence—a sense of morality does not come from the child alone. He also

RIGHT AND WRONG?

Good or bad? ⮕

Psychologists believe that we are not born knowing what's right and wrong, but that we acquire this knowledge as we grow up. Even so, the line between good and bad is not clear-cut.

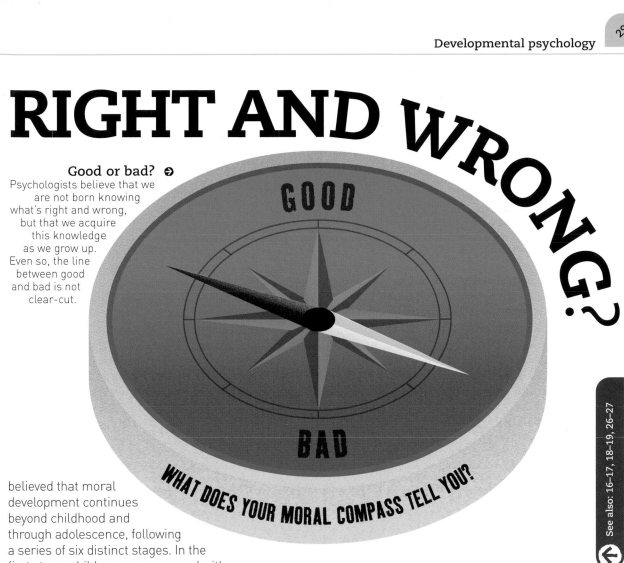

GOOD

BAD

WHAT DOES YOUR MORAL COMPASS TELL YOU?

See also: 16–17, 18–19, 26–27

believed that moral development continues beyond childhood and through adolescence, following a series of six distinct stages. In the first stage, children are concerned with avoiding punishment; in the next, they realize that certain behavior can result in a reward. The third stage involves children trying to conform to what they believe is expected (social norms), in order to be regarded as "good" boys or girls. In the fourth stage, children recognize that there are rules governing behavior laid down by authority figures, such as parents. Moving into adolescence, children begin to understand the reasons for rules and social norms, and how their behavior affects other people, and in the final stage, they form a moral sense based on principles of justice, equality, and reciprocity.

PASSING JUDGMENT

In one moral development study, children watched a puppet show. A ball was passed to one puppet, who sent it back, then passed to another, who ran away with it. The puppets were then put on piles of treats, and each child was asked to take a treat from one of the piles. Most took from the pile of the "naughty" puppet— and one right-minded one-year-old also gave the puppet a smack.

MARY AINSWORTH

1913–1999

Mary Ainsworth is best known for her work on child development, especially mother-and-child relationships. She was born in Ohio but was brought up in Canada, and studied psychology at the University of Toronto. In 1950, she moved to London with her husband, the British psychologist Leonard Ainsworth, and worked with John Bowlby at the Tavistock Clinic. She returned to the United States in 1956 to teach at Johns Hopkins University and the University of Virginia.

RECRUITING TALENT

During World War II, Ainsworth served in the Canadian Women's Army Corps and reached the rank of major. There, she interviewed soldiers to select suitable candidates to become officers. This gave her valuable experience in the techniques of interviewing, keeping records, and interpreting results, and also inspired her interest in the psychology of personality development.

TIME IN AFRICA

In the 1950s, Ainsworth spent a few years in Uganda, Africa, studying the relationships between mothers and their small children in tribal societies. Over a period of up to nine months, she regularly interviewed mothers with babies between the ages of one month and two years. It was here that she developed her ideas about bonding and attachment, and the importance of a mother's sensitivity to her child's needs.

She was an expert in Rorschach tests, a method of assessing personality from the patterns people find in ink blots.

STRANGE SITUATION EXPERIMENT

In 1969, Ainsworth conducted an experiment—later called the Strange Situation—to study the different kinds of attachment between a child and its mother. She observed the reactions of a one-year-old child in a room with toys, first with its mother, then with a stranger as well, then left alone with the stranger, and finally when its mother returned. Different children reacted in various ways depending on the strength of the mother-child relationship.

"**Attachment** is an affection tie that **binds** one person to another in space and **endures** over time."

STAY-AT-HOME MOMS

Ainsworth stressed how important it was for a child to form a secure attachment to a caregiver, but didn't believe that mothers should necessarily have to sacrifice their careers for this. She thought that it was possible for them to combine work and child care, rather than becoming full-time stay-at-home moms. She also felt that more research was needed on the role of fathers and the importance of the bond between father and child.

YOUR SUBJECTIVE AGE IS THE AGE THAT YOU FEEL DEEP DOWN INSIDE. MOST PEOPLE FEEL YOUNGER THAN THEY ARE.

YOUR SOCIAL AGE RELECTS THE ACTIVITIES YOU ENJOY DOING, AS WELL AS YOUR OPINIONS AND ATTITUDES.

Is it never too

AS WE GET OLDER, WE GO THROUGH SEVERAL STAGES OF DEVELOPMENT. AT THE END OF OUR WORKING LIVES, AROUND THE AGE OF 65, WE ENTER A FINAL STAGE, WHICH IN MODERN TIMES CAN LAST FOR 30 YEARS OR MORE. "OLD AGE" IS OFTEN THOUGHT OF AS A PERIOD OF DECLINE, BUT IT MAY ALSO BE A TIME FOR CHANGE AND NEW INTERESTS.

> THERE'S BEEN A **PAST**, AND THERE WILL BE A **FUTURE**. BUT **HERE WE ARE NOW.**
> ROBERT KASTENBAUM

The trouble with old age

Erik Erikson described old age as the last of his eight stages of development—a time for us to take it easy and look back on the earlier stages of our lives. But since he came up with this idea in the 1950s, attitudes toward old age have changed. Many people now live long past their retirement age, so this stage is often seen as a period for further development. Unfortunately, not everybody has the chance to carry on developing in later life. The physical decline of our bodies may prevent us from taking up or continuing with some activities. Some physical problems that occur more often later in life also have a more direct effect on our psychological abilities. A stroke, for example, can damage the brain, causing both physical and mental difficulties. And there are neurodegenerative diseases (diseases that impair the brain or nervous system) that are particularly associated with old age, such as Parkinson's disease and Alzheimer's disease.

Older and wiser

We may become less physically able in old age, but our mental abilities do not necessarily deteriorate. Edward Thorndike believed that, unless we have a

YOUR BIOLOGICAL AGE REFLECTS HOW OLD YOU THINK YOU LOOK, AND HOW OLD YOU THINK OTHER PEOPLE THINK YOU LOOK.

AGE CAN BE MEASURED IN DIFFERENT WAYS.

◉ The Ages of Me

According to psychologist Robert Kastenbaum, we all have three different ages, in addition to our chronological age. Most "old" people think they look older, but feel younger, than they really are.

the world's population is getting older: the proportion of people over age 60 will double in the next 50 years.

See also: 16-17, 42-43

LATE?

neurodegenerative disease, our memories show little decline with age, and older people can continue learning almost as well as young people—just not as quickly. Recent tests show that intelligence also remains relatively unaffected. Although our ability to solve new problems may weaken, our knowledge and wisdom may actually increase. Therefore, our retirement years may be an ideal time to take up new interests, particularly ones that involve mental activity. These might not prevent mental decline, but they have been shown to improve the quality of life as a whole.

As young as you feel

Although we tend to think of people over a certain age as just being "old," there are different stages of old age, and the attitude that old people have toward their age affects the way they live. The psychologist Robert Kastenbaum used a questionnaire called "The Ages of Me" to show that age can be measured in several different ways. Alongside the participants' actual, chronological age, he asked how old they

KARATE KIDS

In a German study, a group of people between the ages of 67 and 93 were given various forms of training. Some did purely mental exercises, others did purely physical training, and a third group learned karate. After several months, it was found that the combination of physical and mental training in karate greatly improved the participants' emotional well-being and quality of life.

thought their bodies looked to themselves and to other people (their biological age). He also asked what age they would associate with their activities, thoughts, opinions, and attitudes (their social age), and how old they felt deep down inside (their subjective age). Not surprisingly, most of them felt that they were younger than their actual age.

LOOK WHO'S TALKING

Babies mimic the babbling of their parents within a few weeks of being born. They also start to recognize language at a very early stage, preferring their parents' speech to that of others. This explains why it is so important for parents to talk to their babies.

HANDS-ON LEARNING

Developmental psychologists have argued that children learn best if they have the freedom to use their imaginations. Montessori schools are based on this ideal, and students are encouraged to learn independently through hands-on activities and discussion with their peers, rather than instruction from teachers.

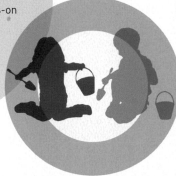

Developmental psychology in the
REAL WORLD

SUPERSTITIOUS BEHAVIOR

Some behaviorist psychologists have suggested that accidental reinforcement of a response can lead to superstitious behavior. For example, if you hit a home run every time you wear a certain pair of socks, you might start to associate wearing the socks with playing well, and will wear them for every game.

OLDER AND WISER

We really do get wiser as we get older. Our capacity for making good decisions takes a long time to develop. The frontal lobes in our brains, which are responsible for decision making, continue to develop until we reach our twenties. So ask a parent or teacher for advice if you're not sure what to do.

Many children's stroller manufacturers are now selling rear-facing designs, following psychological research that showed the importance of parent-child communication in relieving infant stress. If they can see a parent, children feel secure, and are less likely to become distressed.

FEELING SECURE

UNHAPPY HOMES

Psychologists have found that a bad home environment can damage a child's emotional development, often causing poor academic performance and antisocial behavior that can last well into adulthood. Rehabilitation programs for young offenders often focus on their home lives, in order to prevent future criminal behavior.

As we get older, our behavior and skills change. Developmental psychologists study the stages we go through and what influences our development. Their research has had a huge impact on child care and education, and has helped explain certain behaviors by linking them to problems in early life.

BAD INFLUENCE

Some psychologists have argued that violence in movies and video games causes children to become violent themselves. The evidence for this theory is not clear-cut, but concerns have led to the introduction of age ratings for movies and games (for example, PG, PG-13, and R), as a precaution.

DISTANT MEMORIES

Most people cannot remember anything before the age of three. This may be because the way we record and retrieve memories changes at this age. Even so, these early years—when we bond with our caregivers—are crucial to our development, and our experiences at this time can have a lasting impact.

What does my BRAIN do?

Is your MIND different from your BRAIN?

What goes on in your BRAIN?

What can BRAIN DAMAGE TELL us?

What is CONSCIOUSNESS?

DREAM on...

Biological psychology, or biopsychology, combines the physical study of the brain and nervous system—neuroscience—with psychology. Biological psychologists use modern imaging techniques to see what's going on in our brains, and examine how the workings of the brain and nervous system influence our thoughts, feelings, and behavior.

Is your MIND

MUCH OF PSYCHOLOGY IS CONCERNED WITH HOW WE THINK AND BEHAVE—THE WAYS THAT OUR MINDS WORK. BUT THE ACTIVITY OF OUR MINDS TAKES PLACE PHYSICALLY IN OUR BRAINS. IN THE 20TH CENTURY, A BRANCH OF PSYCHOLOGY DEVELOPED THAT LOOKS AT THE CONNECTION BETWEEN THE BIOLOGY OF OUR BRAINS AND OUR BEHAVIOR.

Philosophical minds

Until the development of neuroscience, most people thought of the mind as something separate from the body. This idea originated with the Ancient Greek philosophers, and persisted, even with the advent of science and medicine, in the writings of 17th-century philosopher René Descartes. These philosophers believed that the mind is a kind of "soul," which is capable of thought, while the brain is purely physical and exists to receive information from the senses. Little was known about the physical workings of our brains when psychology first emerged as a science, and many of the early psychologists came from a background of philosophy. As a result, psychology existed for a long time only as the science of the mind and behavior, completely separate from neuroscience—the biological study of the brain.

Mind over matter

Even today, some psychologists believe that the physical makeup of our brains is largely irrelevant to understanding thoughts and behavior, and that any explanation can be provided in terms of our minds. One proponent of this view is the American cognitive

MY MIND CONTROLS MY THOUGHTS...

scientist Jerry Fodor. In the 1980s, he suggested that the mind is made up of many different parts, or "modules," each with its own function—such as retrieving memories or articulating speech. The idea was not entirely new: A century earlier, a pseudoscience called phrenology divided the mind into 27 specialized modules, each associated with an area of the brain. In Fodor's modular theory, however, the mental faculties are not associated with specific parts of the brain, and the modules exist independently from the biological structure of the brain.

THERE IS A GREAT DIFFERENCE BETWEEN MIND AND BODY.

RENÉ DESCARTES

phrenologists claimed to be able to measure intelligence and personality by the size of the bumps on a person's head.

different from your BRAIN?

... BUT MY BRAIN CONTROLS MY MIND.

technology has also allowed us to observe and measure brain activity: For example, electroencephalography (EEG) detects electrical signals, and functional magnetic resonance imaging (fMRI) measures blood flow in different parts of the brain. These techniques have enabled neuroscientists and psychologists to observe which areas of the brain are associated with different behaviors. However, they have also revealed that our brain activity is more complex than previously thought, and that the functions of our minds do not correspond so simply to specific areas of the brain. Certain patterns of brain activity can be associated with different mental states, challenging the idea that the mind is a completely separate entity. Even so, the "brain approach" has not yet provided anything like a full explanation of why we behave the way we do.

while you are awake, your brain generates enough energy to power a light bulb.

Brainpower

Advances in neuroscience allowed scientists to study the structures of the nervous system, and also observe what happens when different parts of the brain are damaged. As a result, certain areas became associated with particular mental faculties. Biological psychology—the "brain approach," as opposed to the "mind approach"—gradually emerged to examine the relationship between the physical workings of our brains and our behavior. Sophisticated scanning

SEDUCTIVE SCANS

A study in 2008 by Deena Weisberg showed that nonscientists are more likely to believe even bad explanations of psychological phenomena if they are accompanied by neuroscientific information and fMRI images. These findings have fueled concerns about presenting neuroscientific evidence to juries in criminal trials.

WE ARE OUR BRAINS.

SUSAN GREENFIELD

What goes on in your **BRAIN?**

OUR NERVOUS SYSTEMS ARE MADE UP OF NERVE CELLS CALLED NEURONS. THESE CELLS COMMUNICATE WITH ONE ANOTHER, TRANSMITTING CHEMICAL AND ELECTRICAL SIGNALS TO AND AROUND OUR BRAINS. MODERN BRAIN-SCANNING TECHNIQUES HAVE ENABLED US TO MEASURE AND OBSERVE THESE SIGNALS INDIRECTLY, AND DISCOVER HOW THEY RELATE TO OUR MENTAL FUNCTIONS AND PROCESSES.

Sending signals

Among the first to study neurons was 19th-century Italian scientist Camillo Golgi. He invented a method of staining the cells, which enabled him to see the paths of signals along them. Santiago Ramón y Cajal built on Golgi's work, and showed that nerve cells are not actually connected, but that they communicate with one another through a structure known as a synapse: Each neuron "fires" an electrical or chemical signal that activates a neighboring neuron. Information can then travel along a chain of neurons, forming a pathway between the brain and other parts of the body. Sensory (receptor) neurons carry information about what we feel, see, hear, taste, and smell via the nervous system to our brains, and motor (effector) neurons carry information from the brain to other parts of our bodies, such as our

NEURONS THAT FIRE TOGETHER, WIRE TOGETHER.

DONALD HEBB

muscles. Drugs such as alcohol affect the brain by altering the nature of this communication process, which is known as synaptic transmission.

Well-known routes

In addition to sending signals to and from the brain, neurons also communicate to form pathways within the brain itself. The patterns of these connections

THE BRAIN'S NEURAL PATHWAYS ARE CONSTANTLY REROUTING.

are associated with different functions of the brain, such as thinking, moving, and speaking. Canadian neuropsychologist Donald Hebb found that when we do something repeatedly, the communication between brain cells is repeated, so the links between them are strengthened. It is then more likely that the cells will communicate with one another along the same pathway in the future. In this way, the brain has "learned" the neural connections associated with that particular activity or mental function. Hebb called these patterns of brain activity "assemblies." These assemblies effectively store the information necessary for the brain to perform various functions. They are not just simple lines of communication along a single line of neurons, but can be complex patterns of interlinked neural pathways. The more often we experience different things at the same time, such as watching a certain movie with a certain friend, the stronger the link between the two pathways of the assembly becomes, causing the two ideas to become associated in our minds. Hebb argued that this is how information is stored in our long-term memories.

PIANO TUNING

In a study of brain activity, volunteers were asked to practice a piano exercise for two hours every day for five days. Afterward, tests showed that the neural pathways in their brains had "reorganized" to give more space to the connections used when playing the exercise. Other participants were asked not to practice, but just to rehearse the exercise in their minds, and their brains went through the same kind of reorganization.

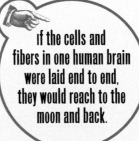

> THE ASTONISHING TANGLE WITHIN OUR HEADS MAKES US WHAT WE ARE.
>
> COLIN BLAKEMORE

Changing tracks

Brain-scanning technology has now enabled neuroscientists to examine synaptic transmission more accurately. Neuroscientist Colin Blakemore has demonstrated that although certain patterns of activity correspond to different functions of the brain, they are not permanent, but change throughout our lives. Over time, as we do different things and live different lives in different circumstances, the neural pathways adapt accordingly in a process known as neuroplasticity, or brain plasticity. Neurons communicate with different neighboring cells to form new pathways in response to changes in behavior or environment. They can even form completely new patterns to replace existing ones if, for example, the brain is damaged.

If the cells and fibers in one human brain were laid end to end, they would reach to the moon and back.

See also: 46–47, 64–65

What can **BRAIN**

EVERY SECOND, THOUSANDS OF SIGNALS ARE BEING PASSED FROM NEURON TO NEURON IN OUR BRAINS. THIS ELECTROCHEMICAL ACTIVITY SPEEDS UP IN DIFFERENT AREAS OF THE BRAIN, DEPENDING ON WHAT WE ARE DOING OR THINKING. WHEN PART OF A BRAIN IS DAMAGED, IT CAN AFFECT SPECIFIC MENTAL FUNCTIONS IN REVEALING WAYS.

> **IF CERTAIN PARTS OF THE BRAIN ARE DAMAGED, OTHER PARTS OF THE BRAIN MAY TAKE ON THE ROLE OF THE DAMAGED PORTION.**
> **KARL LASHLEY**

Speech impediment

In the mid-19th century, French doctor Paul Broca had a patient nicknamed "Tan Tan," who had lost the ability to say anything except the word *tan*. When Tan Tan died, Broca dissected the patient's brain. He found that part of the frontal lobe was malformed, and concluded that this area must be associated with producing speech. A few years later, Carl Wernicke found that damage to another area of the brain affects the ability to understand language. These discoveries marked a turning point in the study of the brain, and showed that

if someone were to poke your brain, you wouldn't feel a thing—the brain itself cannot feel pain.

studying damaged brains can tell us a great deal about the structure of the brain, and how it affects our behavior.

What happens where?

Modern scanning techniques such as fMRI and CT have allowed scientists to observe which parts of the brain are active when people do different things. Just as Broca and Wernicke discovered areas associated with language, neuroscientists have been able to "map" other areas of the brain and their associated functions. But not all of our mental functions are localized in this way. Long-term memory, for example, involves activity in areas all over the brain. A famous case is that of epilepsy patient "HM," who in 1953 had parts of his brain surgically removed. The operation succeeded in controlling his epilepsy, but it severely affected his memory—he could still remember how to do things, but could not recall events. Although HM was widely studied until his death in 2008, it was found that his brain had been more extensively damaged in the operation than previously thought, making it hard to identify which removed part of the brain had been responsible for his memory problems. But brain damage may not always have a lasting effect. Karl Lashley, an American psychologist, suggested that not only do some functions involve several areas of the brain, but when certain areas are damaged, other parts of

PHINEAS GAGE

In 1848, American railroad worker Phineas Gage was in an accident. An iron rod was driven through his head, damaging a large part of the frontal lobe of his brain. Gage survived, but showed a changed personality and uncharacteristic behavior. This was one of the first cases to suggest that functions such as personality are located in specific regions of the brain.

DAMAGE tell us?

the brain may be able to take over these functions. This may explain why some stroke patients, who have lost abilities such as speech or movement, have been able to recover these functions through training.

There are two halves to your brain

Studying the impact of other surgical procedures has also been revealing. The brain consists of two distinct but connected halves—the left and right hemispheres. Roger Sperry discovered that surgically separating the two halves (another treatment for epilepsy) had some interesting side effects. In experiments with split-brain patients, Sperry found that what the left eye sees is processed by the right hemisphere of the brain, and vice versa. Many of his patients were unable to name objects that had been processed by the right side of the brain, but were able to name those processed by the left side. Based on these studies, Sperry suggested that language is controlled by the left side of the brain, whereas the right side has other capabilities.

The premotor cortex plans how and when we should move our bodies.

The primary motor cortex controls the muscles that make our bodies move.

The sensory association cortex analyzes signals from the primary sensory cortex to identify sensations.

The primary sensory cortex receives signals from the surface of our bodies, such as our fingertips.

The visual association cortex processes information, so we can interact with our surroundings.

The prefrontal cortex is associated with intelligence, personality, and making plans and decisions.

When Broca's area is damaged, we can't decide what we want to say, or articulate speech.

The primary auditory cortex receives signals from our ears, and detects volume and pitch.

Wernicke's area is where we make sense of written and spoken language.

The primary visual cortex receives signals from our eyes and identifies basic shapes and colors.

The auditory association cortex analyzes signals from the primary auditory cortex to identify sounds

WHAT HAPPENS WHEN ONE AREA OF THE BRAIN IS DAMAGED?

SANTIAGO RAMÓN Y CAJAL

1852–1934

One of the pioneers of neuroscience, Santiago Ramón y Cajal was born in Navarre, Spain. He was often in trouble for his rebellious behavior as a boy, but eventually settled down to study at the University of Zaragoza medical school, where his father taught anatomy. After serving in the army as a medical officer, he studied the structure of the nervous system, and his work had a great influence on the development of biological psychology.

NAMING THE NEURON

Often referred to as the "father of neuroscience," Ramón y Cajal was the first to describe the nerve cells now known as neurons. He also showed how these cells communicate with one another, transmitting information to various parts of the brain. In 1906, he was the winner (along with Camillo Golgi) of the Nobel Prize in Physiology or Medicine for his work on brain cells.

Ramón y Cajal ended up in prison when he was 11 years old for smashing his neighbor's gate with a homemade cannon.

"The **brain is a world** consisting of a number of **unexplored continents** and great stretches of **unknown territory**."

THE TALENTED ARTIST

From early childhood, Ramón y Cajal showed a talent for painting and drawing, which proved useful in his later work as a neuroscientist. He studied nerve cells before microphotography and imaging were even invented, so he made hundreds of intricately detailed drawings to record what he saw under the microscope. These drawings are still used to illustrate textbooks today.

ALSO KNOWN AS DR. BACTERIA

Ramón y Cajal was a prolific writer. In addition to more than 100 books and articles on scientific subjects, including pathology and the nervous system, he was a well-known author of satirical works, mocking contemporary Spanish society and politics. In 1905, he also published a collection of science-fiction stories under the pen name of Dr. Bacteria.

INVESTIGATING THE UNEXPLAINED

In addition to his work on the physiology of the brain and nervous system, Ramón y Cajal was interested in things that couldn't be so easily explained by science, such as how hypnosis works—he used hypnosis himself to help his wife when she was giving birth. He even wrote a book on hypnosis and the paranormal, which unfortunately went missing after his death, during the Spanish Civil War.

What is

WE ALL KNOW WHAT IT'S LIKE TO BE CONSCIOUS—TO BE AWARE OF OURSELVES AND THE WORLD AROUND US. WE ALSO RECOGNIZE DIFFERENT KINDS OF UNCONSCIOUSNESS, SUCH AS WHEN SOMEONE IS ASLEEP OR UNDER ANESTHESIA. EVEN SO, PSYCHOLOGISTS HAVE STRUGGLED TO EXPLAIN CONSCIOUSNESS IN SCIENTIFIC TERMS.

Streams of thoughts

Early psychologists, including William Wundt and William James, believed that the whole purpose of psychology was to describe and explain our conscious behavior. Since being conscious is a personal experience, the only way in which they could examine consciousness was through introspection—observing what was going on in their own minds. Through this process, James noticed that his conscious thoughts were constantly changing. He might be thinking or doing one thing, when something else sprang to mind; that thought was then soon interrupted by another thought, and so on. However, James also noted the way that these different experiences all seemed to come

A CONSCIOUS IMAGE OF AN APPLE COMBINES LOTS OF ASSOCIATED THOUGHTS.

⬆ **Apple associations**
When we see an apple, our brains not only recognize that it is an apple, but also remind us of everything we associate with the word *apple*—from pies to high-tech gadgets. This, according to Giulio Tononi, is an example of human consciousness.

> WE KNOW THE **MEANING** OF "**CONSCIOUSNESS**" SO LONG AS NO ONE ASKS US TO **DEFINE** IT.
>
> WILLIAM JAMES

CONSCIOUSNESS?

together, flowing from one thought to the next in what he described as a "stream of consciousness."

Levels of consciousness

But what does *consciousness* actually mean? It could mean being aware of our sensations, or of what we are doing and thinking. After all, we say we are doing something "consciously" to distinguish it from automatic actions we do without thinking. Alternatively, *consciousness* may refer simply to being awake, rather than asleep, anesthetized, or knocked out by a blow to the head. Like James, Sigmund Freud was fascinated by consciousness. But instead of trying to explain the state of being conscious, he identified three levels of consciousness: the conscious (what we are aware of), the preconscious (what we can make ourselves aware of), and the unconscious (what we have repressed). Freud's definition of the unconscious is no longer generally accepted, but the different degrees of consciousness continue to interest psychologists.

Scientific solutions

Modern neuroscience suggests that the difference between consciousness and unconsciousness is not clear-cut—even when it is in a coma, the brain is still active. Neuroscientists have observed brain activity in various states of consciousness, helping biological psychologists replace introspective theories of consciousness with more

YOUR **JOYS** AND YOUR SORROWS, YOUR **MEMORIES** AND YOUR AMBITIONS, YOUR SENSE OF PERSONAL IDENTITY AND **FREE WILL**, ARE IN FACT NO MORE THAN THE BEHAVIOR OF A VAST ASSEMBLY OF **NERVE CELLS**.
FRANCIS CRICK

with the amount of signals it receives, and movements it coordinates, your brain is more powerful than a supercomputer.

scientific explanations. The biologist Francis Crick compared the brain activity of healthy people and those in a persistent vegetative state. He found that, in the conscious brains, there was more activity in the area known as the prefrontal cortex than in the unconscious brains, and concluded that it was this part of the brain that is associated with consciousness. A more recent theory, proposed by neuroscientist Giulio Tononi, is that consciousness is a result of the interconnection of structures in various parts of our brains, linking the information from all our senses, memories, and thoughts. He explained his idea using the analogy of a camera taking a picture of an apple. The image the camera receives is composed of many different pixels, but the camera treats each pixel separately and does not see the apple as a whole. In contrast, our brains can make the connections between the pixels both to give us a picture of the apple in our minds, and to remind us of everything we associate with the idea of an apple. Thus, it is not just the amount of activity in our brains, but the degree of its interconnectivity that determines our level of consciousness.

See also: 40–41, 48–49, 50–51

VILAYANUR RAMACHANDRAN

1951–

Neuroscientist Vilayanur Ramachandran was born in Tamil Nadu, India. His father worked for the United Nations, so the family moved frequently, and Ramachandran went to school in Madras and Bangkok, Thailand. He studied medicine in Madras, then moved to England, earning a PhD from Cambridge University. He worked as a researcher at Oxford University before settling in the United States. He is now a professor in the Department of Psychology at the University of California.

SEEING THINGS

Ramachandran has taken a somewhat unorthodox approach to neuroscience. Rather than using the latest imaging technology to examine how the brain works, he tends to work from experiments and observation. Some of his earliest research was on the way our brains process visual information, and he invented a number of visual effects and optical illusions that increased our understanding of how we perceive what we see.

MISSING LIMBS

Ramachandran is probably best known for his work on "phantom limbs"— when amputees continue to feel sensation from a removed limb. To help relieve the discomfort these patients sometimes feel, he invented a mirror box, which reflects the image of an existing limb to create the illusion that the amputated limb has been replaced. This gives patients a visual image to associate with their sensations.

> "Any **ape** can reach for a **banana**, but only **humans** can **reach for the stars**."

INVESTIGATING IMPOSTORS

One way Ramachandran examines the working of our brains is by studying people with unusual neurological syndromes. People suffering from the Capgras delusion, for example, believe that a relative has been replaced by an impostor. Ramachandran thinks that this is because the area of their brains that recognizes faces, the temporal cortex, is disconnected from the area involved with emotional responses.

In 2011, *Time* magazine listed him as one of "the most influential people in the world."

CROSSED WIRES

Some people may perceive letters, numbers, or even days of the week as having different colors, or even personalities. Known as synesthesia, this is an automatic and involuntary experience, which Ramachandran explains in terms of an interconnection between normally unrelated regions of the brain—when one area is stimulated by incoming information, it also triggers a response in the other area.

DREAM on...

REVEALING DREAMS
FREUD BELIEVED THAT WHEN WE SLEEP, WE ACT OUT THE HIDDEN DESIRES AND FEARS THAT WE REPRESS IN OUR WAKING LIVES.

SLEEPING IS AN ESSENTIAL PART OF OUR DAILY LIVES. WITHOUT REGULAR SLEEP, WE STRUGGLE TO FUNCTION WELL PHYSICALLY OR MENTALLY. BY STUDYING THE ACTIVITY OF SLEEPING PEOPLE'S BRAINS, AND BY OBSERVING WHAT HAPPENS WHEN SLEEP PATTERNS ARE DISRUPTED, PSYCHOLOGISTS ARE BEGINNING TO UNDERSTAND WHY SLEEP IS SO IMPORTANT.

yawning is contagious—even reading the word "yawn" can set people off.

The stages of sleep

Some people believe that sleep is simply an opportunity for our bodies and minds to recover after activity—when we are tired, we sleep, and wake up feeling refreshed. But there may be other reasons for sleep, too. Scientists have discovered that in a typical night we go through four or five cycles of sleep, each lasting about 90 minutes. In each cycle, there are four increasingly deep stages of sleep. During the three stages of non-rapid-eye-movement (NREM) sleep, our muscles relax and our brain activity, breathing, and heart rate slow down, but we may still toss and turn. In the fourth, rapid-eye-movement (REM) stage, our breathing and heart rate speed up,

WITHOUT THE **BIOLOGICAL CLOCKS** IN OUR BRAINS, OUR LIVES WOULD BE **CHAOTIC**, OUR ACTIONS DISORGANIZED.

COLIN BLAKEMORE

but our muscles are immobilized, so we cannot move around. Although they are closed, our eyes move rapidly, and our brains behave almost as if we were awake. This stage is when we dream.

What's the point of dreaming?

Our brains don't "shut down" while we are asleep. In fact, during REM sleep they are as active as when we are awake. It seems that, rather than being in a state of unconsciousness, we move into a different kind of consciousness—the time when we dream—and many psychologists believe this is the most important purpose of sleep. Sigmund Freud and his followers believed that dreams allow us to do and say things in our minds that we repress in our waking lives. He saw examining our dreams as a way of accessing our hidden unconscious minds. Other psychologists think that dreams give us an opportunity to practice things

TEEN TIME SHIFT

Studies suggest that teenagers do less well at school in the mornings because they are still in need of the final stages of sleep. Neuroscientist Russell Foster explained that, between the ages of 10 and 20, our body clocks shift, possibly for hormonal reasons. This means that we need to get up about two hours later than everyone else.

Most people dream for one or two hours each night, and have up to seven dreams.

CAPTURE THE MEANING OF YOUR DREAMS...

FILING SYSTEM
WE MAY USE OUR DREAMS TO ORGANIZE OUR THOUGHTS AND MEMORIES, MAKING ROOM FOR NEW INFORMATION.

FIGHT OR FLIGHT
REVONSUO ARGUED THAT, IN OUR DREAMS, WE REHEARSE THINGS WE NEED TO DO IN REAL LIFE—SUCH AS ESCAPING DANGER.

in our minds that we can later use in our waking lives. For example, the scientist Antti Revonsuo showed that the fight-or-flight area of the brain is more active than normal during REM sleep. Many people solve problems in their dreams, and creative artists are often inspired to write, compose, or paint by ideas that come to them in their sleep. Alternatively, we may use dreams to organize our thoughts and ideas, uncluttering our minds and making room for new information.

Watching our body clocks
Just as we follow a pattern during our sleep, we also have an internal "body clock" that tells us when we need to sleep. Although we normally follow the natural cycle of night and day, the rhythm of sleep and wakefulness has its own pattern. In general, we tend to be awake for 16 hours, then sleep for eight, but we can live happily with other rhythms. In one experiment, French cave explorer and scientist Michel Siffre spent seven months underground, completely unaware of the changing night and day above. Following solely his biological body clock, he settled into a pattern of a 25-hour day. However, if we are deprived of sleep for long periods of time, we feel physically and mentally unwell, and are more prone to accidents. In fact, sleep deprivation is sometimes used as a method of torture, and can result in death. Modern life often disrupts natural sleep patterns, too, through jet lag, night shifts, or simply longer working hours. These demands mean that most of us are not getting as much sleep as we need.

CREATIVE STREAK
MUSICIANS AND ARTISTS FIND INSPIRATION IN THEIR DREAMS FOR NEW COMPOSITIONS, AND WE ALSO SOLVE PROBLEMS.

See also: 46–47

NEURON LIGHT SHOW

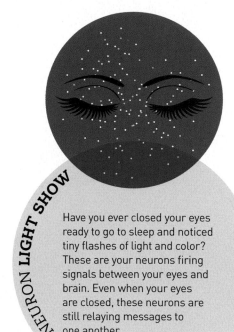

Have you ever closed your eyes ready to go to sleep and noticed tiny flashes of light and color? These are your neurons firing signals between your eyes and brain. Even when your eyes are closed, these neurons are still relaying messages to one another.

MAGNETIC FIELDS

Since neurons work by transmitting electrical signals, they can be disrupted by strong magnetic fields. Biological psychologists have used this technique to study how different parts of the brain function. Effects include temporary loss of speech, hallucinations, and even religious experiences.

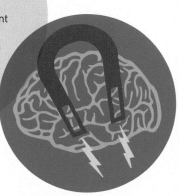

Biological psychology in the
REAL WORLD

AT YOUR BRAINIEST

Your parents have simpler brains than you. The number of new connections in our brains peaks when we are about nine years old, and then decreases until our twenties, when it stabilizes. Our brains are more malleable in our early years—this is why children find it easier to learn a new language than adults.

STILL FAST ASLEEP

Sometimes people get up, walk around, and even clean the house when they are still asleep. Contrary to popular belief, sleepwalkers aren't acting out their dreams or unconscious desires. Biological psychologists have shown that sleepwalking occurs during non-rapid-eye-movement (NREM) sleep—when we are not dreaming.

Studies have found that teenagers have a different biological clock from adults, and that they would benefit from getting up two hours later than everyone else. This has led some psychologists to argue that school shouldn't start so early in the morning.

INTERNAL CLOCK

SAFETY FIRST

Imagine putting Jell-O in a box with sharp insides, and shaking it. This is what happens when you hit your head very hard. Biological psychologists have found that serious blows to the head can have a huge impact on our behavior and abilities. Their work supports calls for stricter laws requiring cyclists to wear helmets.

Biological psychology links our thoughts, feelings, and behavior to the physical workings of our brains. Using brain-scanning technology to study the activity of the brain, biological psychologists try to offer scientific explanations for behavior resulting from brain abnormalities and damage.

Our brains respond to the body movements and positions of other people. Mirror neurons activate when we observe specific actions, and help us mimic movements and learn new skills, such as dancing or hitting a winning shot in tennis. This is why we learn best by copying the actions of an expert.

MIRROR, MIRROR

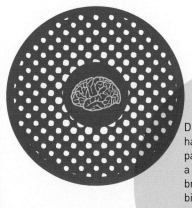

NO WAY THROUGH

Drugs that affect our brains have to be made of very small particles in order to pass through a membrane called the blood-brain barrier. Working with biological psychologists, scientists are trying to help drug addicts by creating chemicals that bind to drugs, making them too large to get through the barrier.

How does my MIND work?

What is KNOWLEDGE?

Decisions, decisions, DECISIONS

Why do you REMEMBER stuff?

How are memories STORED?

Don't TRUST your memory

Information OVERLOAD?

Watch your LANGUAGE!

Are you FOOLING yourself?

How do we MAKE SENSE of the world?

Don't BELIEVE your eyes

Cognitive psychology is the study of mental processes, rather than human behavior. Cognitive psychologists examine the way our minds deal with information coming from our senses—such as how we make sense of what we see and hear, and how we learn language and store things in our memories.

What is

WHAT WE KNOW—KNOWLEDGE—IS MADE UP OF WHAT WE HAVE LEARNED ABOUT THE WORLD AROUND US AND HOW WE CAN LIVE IN IT. WHEN WE LEARN SOMETHING, SUCH AS A FACT OR HOW TO DO A TASK, WE STORE THAT INFORMATION IN OUR MEMORY. THE INFORMATION THAT WE HAVE STORED AND CAN REMEMBER IS WHAT WE CALL KNOWLEDGE.

Don't stick to the facts

For a long time, it was thought that knowledge consisted of nothing but facts, and traditional teaching methods focused on getting students to memorize those facts, often through constant repetition. But as psychology emerged as a science in the 20th century, ideas of knowledge began to change. The way we learn, and the way we remember things, became major branches of study for psychologists, challenging the notion that knowledge is simply remembering facts, and giving a new perspective on the role of the learner and the teacher in acquiring knowledge. Even so, early behaviorist psychologists continued to think of knowledge as a collection of facts, which could be learned through conditioning. Some, particularly John B. Watson, believed that almost anything could be taught in this way. But others, including Edward Thorndike and B. F. Skinner, realized that learning is not just a question of collecting and storing knowledge from the outside world; the learner also has a part to play, by actively exploring his or her environment and learning by experience.

 shorter classes could help us learn more effectively—our brains tend to shut down if they are overloaded.

⊕ **Snowball**

The way we gain knowledge is similar to the way a snowball grows as it rolls down a snow-covered hill. We search for meaning in the information we gather, which helps us remember it better. We learn best if we experience things firsthand, rather than just gathering facts.

KNOWLEDGE?

We need to experience things

Developmental psychologists, such as Jean Piaget and Lev Vygotsky, took this idea further. They noted that children build up their knowledge step by step, going over ideas in more and more detail and making connections with other ideas. This involves actively and continually experiencing things, rather than getting knowledge secondhand, so simply being told or shown something by a teacher may not always be the best way to learn. Knowledge is more likely to stick if we're encouraged to participate in the learning process—for example, by making a cake, rather than just reading a recipe—and then to make sense of the information we discover.

> **KNOWLEDGE IS A PROCESS, NOT A PRODUCT.**
> **JEROME BRUNER**

Making sense of stuff

One of the first psychologists, Hermann Ebbinghaus, showed in 1885 that we remember things better if they have some meaning for us. A poem, he found, is easier to remember than a random set of letters.

More recently, cognitive psychologist Jerome Bruner realized that because we need to make sense of information in order to learn it, acquiring knowledge involves thinking and reasoning as well as our senses and memory. Learning is not just what we do to gain knowledge; it is also a mental process, in which we find meaning in the information gathered and connect it to other knowledge. And because learning is a continuous process, our knowledge is continually changing.

GATHERING KNOWLEDGE IS A CONTINUOUS PROCESS.

See also: 16–17, 24–25

Decisions,

THROUGHOUT OUR LIVES, WE ARE FACED WITH DIFFICULT CHOICES. WE CONSTANTLY HAVE TO SOLVE PROBLEMS AND MAKE DECISIONS, AND TO DO THAT WE NEED TO USE OUR ABILITY TO REASON—TO THINK ABOUT A PROBLEM AND MAKE SENSE OF IT. THIS PROCESS OF RATIONAL THOUGHT GIVES US THE INFORMATION WE NEED TO MAKE THE RIGHT CHOICE.

ANIMALS SOLVE PROBLEMS IN THEIR MINDS FIRST.
WOLFGANG KÖHLER

Bananas in awkward places

Reasoning, or thinking about a problem, is one of the mental processes that most interests cognitive psychologists. But earlier psychologists also studied the way we go about solving problems. From 1913 to 1920, German psychologist Wolfgang Köhler was the director of a research institute that was home to a colony of chimpanzees. He set the chimpanzees various tasks, such as reaching bananas in awkward places, and observed how they found solutions. When the chimps realized they couldn't reach the food, they tried standing on boxes or using sticks. Köhler noticed that, after trying out various methods, the chimpanzees stopped and thought about what they had discovered. He concluded that they were reasoning about what did and didn't work, and recognizing patterns and making connections that would help them solve similar problems in the future.

Mental maps to find solutions

At the time Köhler was observing the process of reasoning in his chimpanzees, most psychologists were more interested in behavior than mental processes. Behaviorist psychologists believed that we (and other animals) learned simply by stimulus and response. Some, however, realized that there was more to it than that. Edward Tolman, for example, explained that we do explore the world through a

process of trial and error, learning which things we do give us a reward and which don't, but we also think about these things and build up a "mental map" of the world around us. We can then use this map to help us solve problems and make decisions.

Illogical decisions

Rational thought—reasoning—is crucial in helping us understand problems and gain insights into solving them. It's what allows us to make sensible decisions, choosing what to do based on the evidence of our experience. But the Israeli psychologists Daniel Kahneman and Amos Tversky warned that our reasoning is not always reliable, and that we sometimes make decisions that seem to be rational, but are actually based on mistaken reasoning, or no reasoning at all. From our experience, we build a set of general "rules of thumb" that we can refer to whenever we make a decision. However, these guidelines are mainly based on a small amount of personal experience and may not provide an accurate picture. They may also be influenced by our personal opinions and beliefs. And although they help us make decisions more quickly and easily, without having to examine the statistical evidence in detail, they often lead us to make irrational decisions—even though

AFTER SEEING A LONG RUN OF RED ON THE ROULETTE WHEEL, MOST PEOPLE WRONGLY BELIEVE THAT BLACK IS NOW DUE.
DANIEL KAHNEMAN AND AMOS TVERSKY

decisions, DECISIONS

Losing a night's sleep can lead us to make decisions that are much riskier than normal.

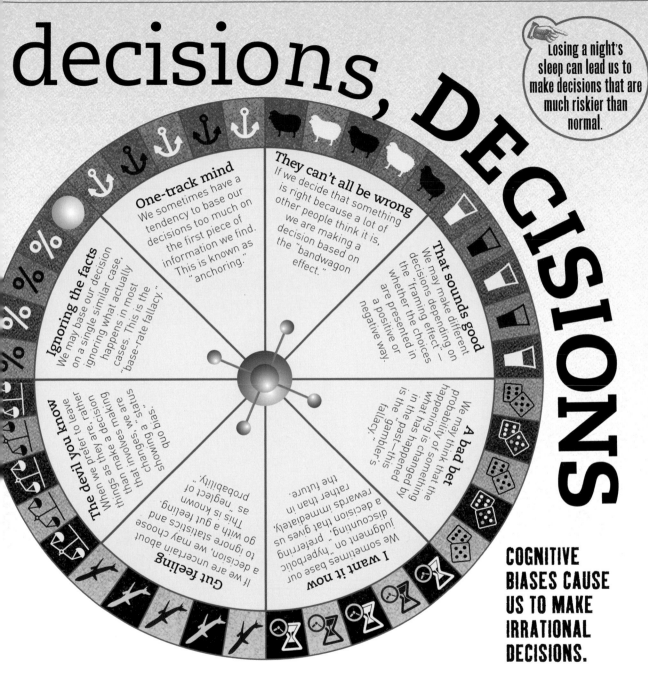

One-track mind
We sometimes have a tendency to base our decisions too much on the first piece of information we find. This is known as "anchoring."

They can't all be wrong
If we decide that something is right because a lot of other people think it is, we are making a decision based on the "bandwagon effect."

Ignoring the facts
We may base our decision on a single similar case, ignoring what actually happens in most cases. This is the "base-rate fallacy."

That sounds good
We may make different decisions depending on the "framing effect"— whether the choices are presented in a positive or negative way.

The devil you know
When we prefer to leave things as they are, rather than make a making decision that involves a change, we are showing "status quo bias."

A bad bet
We may think probability of something happening is changing when what has happened in the "past"—this is the "gambler's fallacy."

Gut feeling
If we are uncertain about a decision, we may choose to ignore statistics and go with a gut feeling. This is known as "neglect of probability."

I want it now
We sometimes base our judgment on "hyperbolic discounting," preferring a decision that gives us rewards immediately, rather than in the future.

COGNITIVE BIASES CAUSE US TO MAKE IRRATIONAL DECISIONS.

we believe they are rational. Kahneman and Tversky identified several different types of faulty reasoning we use in making decisions, which they called "cognitive biases." Cognitive biases are based largely on our personal experiences, so the irrational decisions we make because of them may serve

us well enough in our day-to-day lives. But when it comes to important decision making, especially in situations that are new to us, we should be aware of how such bias can mislead us. Understanding these common faults in reasoning can help us avoid making dangerous or costly mistakes.

Why do you REMEMBER

AS WE LEARN THINGS, WE STORE A REPRESENTATION OF THE INFORMATION IN OUR MINDS AS MEMORIES, AND WHEN WE REMEMBER THINGS, WE ARE RETRIEVING THAT REPRESENTATION. BUT RECALLING A MEMORY ISN'T ALWAYS EASY, AND WE REMEMBER SOME THINGS BETTER THAN OTHERS. OFTEN, WE NEED SOME KIND OF CUE TO TRIGGER A PARTICULAR MEMORY.

How memory works

Psychologists have tried to understand human memory ever since psychology started to be studied as a science. One of the first true psychologists, Hermann Ebbinghaus, noticed that even when we think we have learned something, a day later we often find we have forgotten most of it. In his innovative experiments, he proved that we remember things better if we take more time to learn them. He also found that random lists of words or numbers are trickier to remember than something that has meaning to us, and

Where was I when...?
Memories of events and facts are connected, so we find it easier to recall things if we can remember where and when we learned them.

Rudely interrupted
When what we are doing is interrupted, our minds tend to hang on to that activity, and we recall it better than things that no longer need our attention.

WHY YOU REMEMBER SOME THINGS BETTER THAN OTHERS

Flashbulb memories
Dramatic and highly emotional events are burned into our memories, and we can recall very clearly what we were doing when they happened.

In the mood
Memories are associated with how we feel when we learn something, and we tend to recall memories that match the mood we are in now.

See also: 64–65, 66–67

stuff?

that we tend to recall the beginning or end of a series better than the middle. Later psychologists continued to investigate the idea that how and when we learn something affects how well we remember it. For example, Bluma Zeigarnik had heard that waiters could recall details of orders that had not yet been paid for better than orders they had completed. Intrigued, she did an experiment in which participants were given simple puzzles to do. They were interrupted during about half of these tasks. Later, the participants found it easier to recall details of the interrupted puzzles. Like the waiters' orders, if a task lacks closure, it will stick in our minds.

Give us a cue

Cognitive psychologists like Zeigarnik saw memory as a kind of information-processing system. Endel Tulving said that we have different kinds of memory to store different types of information: memory of facts and knowledge, memory of events and experiences, and memory of how to do things. He also described memory as two separate processes: storing information in long-term memory (learning), and retrieving information (recalling). These two processes, he saw, are connected. For instance, if we are reminded of what was happening at the time we put information into long-term memory, it helps us recall it. This is an example of how a clue or "memory cue" can trigger the retrieval of information, or "jog our memory."

Memory-altering moods

Our mood can also help us recall particular memories. Gordon H. Bower believed that "events and emotions are

> **FLASHBULB MEMORIES ARE FIRED BY EVENTS OF HIGH EMOTIONALITY.**
> ROGER BROWN

stored in memory together," and that our memories of events and experiences are particularly linked to the mood we are in. Thus, when we are happy, we tend to recall things that happened when we were in a good mood, and when we are unhappy, we tend to remember things that happened when we were in a bad mood. Roger Brown called extreme examples of mood-dependent memory "flashbulb memories"—meaning that we can often recall exactly what we were doing when something dramatic or highly emotional happened to us, such as hearing news of the September 11 terrorist attacks, or the death of a friend or relative.

> You are more likely to remember your dreams if you are woken up while dreaming.

BADDELEY'S DIVERS

In an experiment devised by Alan Baddeley, a group of divers were asked to memorize lists of words. They learned some of these on dry land, and some underwater. When asked to recall these lists, the divers remembered the words learned underwater better if they went underwater again, and the others better if they stayed on dry land. This is an example of context-dependent memory.

ELIZABETH LOFTUS

1944–

Born in Los Angeles in 1944, Elizabeth Loftus studied math at the University of California, intending to become a teacher. But, after taking classes in psychology, she changed career paths and completed a PhD in psychology at Stanford University. It was there that she first took an interest in long-term memory—a subject that has defined her career.

CAR CRASH

One of Loftus's first studies tested the reliability of eyewitness testimony in criminal court cases, and whether or not it can be influenced by leading questions. Participants were shown film clips of car accidents, and then asked to estimate how fast the cars were going. People gave higher estimates when asked how fast the cars "smashed" into one another than if they were asked how fast they "bumped" into one another.

FALSE MEMORIES

In the 1990s, George Franklin was convicted of a murder that had happened 20 years earlier, based on a memory his daughter had recovered under hypnosis. Loftus argued that although the woman sincerely believed her memory, it was false and had arisen from suggestion during hypnotherapy. The conviction was overturned.

"Do you swear to tell the **truth**, the **whole truth**, or whatever it is you **think you remember**?"

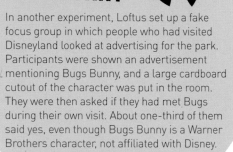

MEETING BUGS BUNNY

In another experiment, Loftus set up a fake focus group in which people who had visited Disneyland looked at advertising for the park. Participants were shown an advertisement mentioning Bugs Bunny, and a large cardboard cutout of the character was put in the room. They were then asked if they had met Bugs during their own visit. About one-third of them said yes, even though Bugs Bunny is a Warner Brothers character, not affiliated with Disney.

Loftus has advised on the reliability of eyewitness testimony in more than 250 court cases, including the trial of singer Michael Jackson.

BREAKING BAD HABITS

Loftus started to wonder if implanting false memories could be used to influence behavior such as eating habits. In an experiment, she led participants to believe that strawberry ice cream had made them sick as children. A week later, many participants had developed detailed memories of the incident and an aversion to ice cream. Loftus thinks this method could be used in the fight against teenage obesity.

How are memories

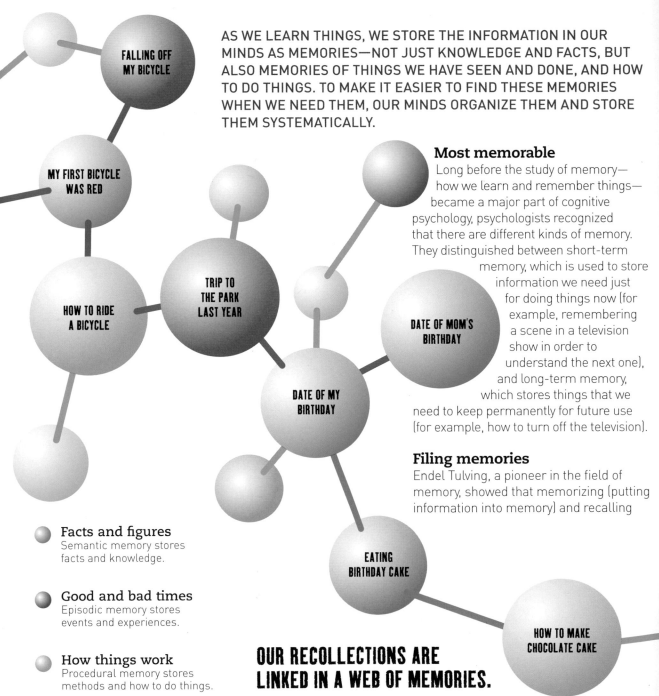

AS WE LEARN THINGS, WE STORE THE INFORMATION IN OUR MINDS AS MEMORIES—NOT JUST KNOWLEDGE AND FACTS, BUT ALSO MEMORIES OF THINGS WE HAVE SEEN AND DONE, AND HOW TO DO THINGS. TO MAKE IT EASIER TO FIND THESE MEMORIES WHEN WE NEED THEM, OUR MINDS ORGANIZE THEM AND STORE THEM SYSTEMATICALLY.

FALLING OFF MY BICYCLE

MY FIRST BICYCLE WAS RED

HOW TO RIDE A BICYCLE

TRIP TO THE PARK LAST YEAR

DATE OF MOM'S BIRTHDAY

DATE OF MY BIRTHDAY

EATING BIRTHDAY CAKE

HOW TO MAKE CHOCOLATE CAKE

Most memorable

Long before the study of memory—how we learn and remember things—became a major part of cognitive psychology, psychologists recognized that there are different kinds of memory. They distinguished between short-term memory, which is used to store information we need just for doing things now (for example, remembering a scene in a television show in order to understand the next one), and long-term memory, which stores things that we need to keep permanently for future use (for example, how to turn off the television).

Filing memories

Endel Tulving, a pioneer in the field of memory, showed that memorizing (putting information into memory) and recalling

Facts and figures
Semantic memory stores facts and knowledge.

Good and bad times
Episodic memory stores events and experiences.

How things work
Procedural memory stores methods and how to do things.

OUR RECOLLECTIONS ARE LINKED IN A WEB OF MEMORIES.

STORED?

REMEMBERING IS MENTAL TIME TRAVEL.

ENDEL TULVING

See also: 60–61, 66–67

(retrieving memories from storage) are two different, but connected, processes. We put a vast amount of information into our memory store, and need to locate and access specific memories at different times. If the information were stored at random, this would be almost impossible, so these memories must be organized in some way. Tulving suggested that we have three different kinds of memory stores: semantic memory, which stores facts and knowledge; episodic memory, which records events and experiences; and procedural memory, which reminds us how to do things. Each of these stores is further subdivided to make information even more accessible. This means that, rather than having to search the whole of our memory to recall something, our minds can be told which general area to look in. For instance, if the episodic memory store organizes memories of events according to when and where they happened, our minds can recall specific memories by taking us back to that particular time and place. In a similar way, Tulving described the semantic memory store as being organized into categories. In experiments, he found that participants trying to recall a word from a random list could have their memories jogged by naming a category: Words such as

Dark chocolate is one of several "superfoods" that improve blood flow to the brain and may help us form memories.

cat and spoon could be recalled by giving cues such as animal and utensil. Later psychologists pointed out that things can belong to more than one category—for example, the word apple could equally well be organized under the category fruit or company. Rather than listing distinct categories, they described memory as a "web" of interconnected memories.

In our own words

British psychologist Frederic Bartlett offered a slightly different explanation of how our memory store is organized. He asked a number of students to read a complicated story, and later asked them to retell it. Although they could remember the general shape of the story, there were parts that they couldn't recall. Bartlett found that the students changed details that did not fit with their own experiences, so the story made more sense to them. He concluded that we all have what he called a "schema"—a set of ideas shaped by our experience—which provides a framework for our memories. Although this helps us store some memories, it is very difficult to retain those that don't fit in with our individual schemas.

REMEMBERING IS AN IMAGINATIVE RECONSTRUCTION BUILT OUT OF OUR ATTITUDE TOWARDS PAST EXPERIENCES.

FREDERIC BARTLETT

Don't TRUST

OUR MEMORIES CAN OFTEN LET US DOWN. SOMETIMES, THERE ARE THINGS WE'RE SURE WE HAVE STORED IN OUR MEMORY BUT JUST CAN'T RECALL, SUCH AS THE NAME OF A CELEBRITY OR THE ANSWER TO A SIMPLE QUESTION ON A TEST. AT OTHER TIMES, WE REMEMBER THINGS WRONGLY, EVEN THOUGH WE BELIEVE WE'VE GOT THEM RIGHT.

strangely enough, chewing gum can improve your ability to remember things.

Limited storage space

One of the main problems with memory is that there is so much information coming into our minds, and our memories just don't have the capacity to store everything we experience. Even if they did, they would be cluttered up with huge amounts of useless information, making it more difficult to retrieve the things we want. Consequently, our minds label some memories as "junk" and let some of the older ones fade away. Most of the time, this system works pretty well, allowing us to store and recall the most useful facts and experiences. But sometimes we find

that our minds have stowed some information we need in a place where it's difficult to get at. We then can't recall what we need to know, or can only recall part of it, and may even get it confused with other information. American psychologist Daniel Schacter listed seven different ways in which our memories can let us down, and called them the "seven sins of memory."

It's on the tip of my tongue

Schacter realized that there are various reasons for not remembering things. Sometimes, we know we know something, but we can't access the memory. This

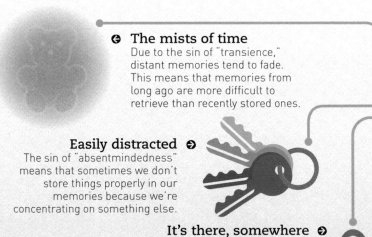

The mists of time
Due to the sin of "transience," distant memories tend to fade. This means that memories from long ago are more difficult to retrieve than recently stored ones.

Easily distracted
The sin of "absentmindedness" means that sometimes we don't store things properly in our memories because we're concentrating on something else.

It's there, somewhere
Sometimes, we know we know something, but we just can't recall it. This is often because another memory is getting in the way, committing the sin of "blocking."

7 WAYS YOUR MEMORY CAN LET YOU DOWN

your memory

might be because it was stored a long time ago, or badly, or because other memories have gotten in the way—especially the kind of irritating or upsetting memory that we just can't get out of our minds. Very often, however, we think we remember something, but in reality our minds are getting different memories confused. Even a vivid memory of an event can get mixed up with another memory, so that what we remember is different from what actually happened. Our recollections of the past are also influenced by the way we think and feel now.

Distorted memories

We can recall memories fairly accurately most of the time, particularly of things that are important to us. It tends to be details that we get wrong, such as who said what, or where and when something

> **PEOPLE CAN COME TO BELIEVE THINGS THAT NEVER REALLY HAPPENED.**
> ELiZABETH LOFTUS

happened. Experiments by Elizabeth Loftus have shown that our memories of events are often inaccurate, even though we believe them to be true. Factors such as leading questions, emotions, and subsequent events can affect the way we recall traumatic events, such as witnessing a crime or a car crash. Her work has called into question the validity of some eyewitness testimony in court cases. More controversially, she has also challenged the "false memories" of some people claiming to have been the victims of abuse when they were children.

Now and then
When we recall a memory, our opinions and emotions may be very different from when we stored that memory. When our present mood and thoughts color our recollections, this is the sin of "bias."

Who said that?
We commit the sin of "misattribution" when the information is right, but the source is wrong. We think that we saw something on the news, for example, when in fact we heard it from a friend.

Leading questions
Memories can be influenced by how they are recalled. We may alter a memory to match whatever prompted it, such as a leading question—the sin of "suggestibility."

Can't forget
There are some memories that we just can't forget. The sin of "persistence" means that distressing or embarrassing events keep coming back to us.

POST-TRAUMATIC STRESS

An extreme example of the persistence of unwanted memories is seen in post-traumatic stress disorder. For instance, soldiers who have returned from action often cannot forget the horrific experiences they have had. These memories continue to haunt them, getting in the way of their memories of good things, and making it difficult to settle back into everyday life back home.

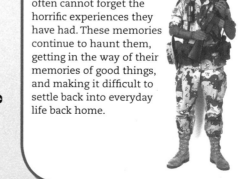

See also: 60–61, 62–63, 64–65

Information OVERLOAD?

WHILE WE ARE AWAKE, OUR SENSES ARE CONSTANTLY PICKING UP INFORMATION ABOUT THE WORLD AROUND US. THERE IS AN ENORMOUS AMOUNT FOR US TO SEE, HEAR, SMELL, AND TOUCH—SO MUCH INFORMATION THAT OUR MINDS CANNOT TAKE IT ALL IN. INSTEAD, OUR MINDS SELECT WHAT WE NEED TO FOCUS OUR ATTENTION ON AND FILTER OUT THE REST.

Pay attention

Some tasks involve dealing with a lot of incoming information and figuring out what is important. In addition to flying a plane, a pilot has to watch dials and gauges, and listen to instructions from air traffic control and other crew members through headphones. Donald Broadbent, a psychologist who served in Britain's Royal Air Force during World War II, studied how pilots dealt with all this information.

> **OUR MIND** CAN BE CONCEIVED AS A **RADIO** RECEIVING **MANY CHANNELS** AT ONCE.
>
> **DONALD BROADBENT**

He devised experiments in which participants wearing headphones heard different information in each ear. They were asked to concentrate on one set of information, and Broadbent found they did not register the content of the other channel. He concluded that we can only listen to one voice at a time. When we are receiving information through many channels, our mind effectively closes all but the channel that we need to focus our attention on.

Tune in, block out

Broadbent's study of attention was similar to the work of information scientist Colin Cherry. Cherry was interested in how we select which channel of information to pay attention to, and separate it from other incoming information. Likening it to the way we listen to just one conversation at a noisy party, he

WE CAN ONLY LISTEN TO ONE VOICE AT A TIME.

⊘ Are you listening?
People in a crowded room tend to focus their attention on one conversation, blocking out the surrounding noise. But we are quick to tune in to another conversation if we hear something of interest.

"multitasking" is actually just switching between different tasks— our brains juggle them, handling one at a time.

called this the "cocktail party problem." He found that we "tune in" to things such as a particular tone of voice, and our minds block out what they consider background noise. Surprisingly, he also found that if someone in another conversation mentions our name or something that might be of interest to us, our mind switches focus. Broadbent noticed a similar effect with pilots, who switched focus from one channel to another when an urgent message came through. So even though we're not focusing on it, our ears are still picking up information from what is filtered out, and our minds can identify key messages.

Magical number seven
All this information, Broadbent suggested, goes into a short-term memory store, where just one channel is selected for attention and the rest is filtered out to prevent a bottleneck. George Armitage Miller described this short-term memory as a place where information is processed, especially before it is stored in long-term

SHORT-TERM MEMORY CAN HOLD ABOUT SEVEN ITEMS AT ONE TIME.
GEORGE ARMITAGE MILLER

memory. Rather than examining how the information is selected for attention, he wanted to know how much information this short-term, or "working," memory could hold. In experiments playing a series of tones or displaying a number of dots briefly on a screen, he found that we can only take in about seven things at a time, and concluded that the capacity of working memory is limited to about seven items, which he called the "magical number."

INVISIBLE APE
In a study examining attention, participants watched a video of people passing a basketball, and were asked to count the number of passes. Most participants were so engrossed in counting the passes that they failed to spot a person dressed in a gorilla costume walking right through the center of the scene.

DONALD BROADBENT

1926–1993

A hugely influential psychologist, Donald Broadbent's regular television and radio appearances helped popularize psychology. He was born in Birmingham, England, and left school to join the Royal Air Force during World War II. He then studied psychology at Cambridge and worked at the university's Applied Psychology Unit, becoming its director in 1958. In 1974, he moved to Oxford University, where he worked until his retirement in 1991.

YOU CAN ONLY LISTEN TO ONE VOICE AT A TIME

Broadbent is best known for his work on how we focus our attention. From his experience in the Royal Air Force, he recognized the problems faced by pilots and air traffic controllers who have to deal with lots of incoming information simultaneously, and developed experiments to show that we can only listen to one voice at a time.

Broadbent was born in England but always considered himself a Welshman, since he spent much of his early life in Wales.

"The **test** of a psychological theory lies in its **practical applications**."

PSYCHOLOGY SHOULD SOLVE REAL LIFE PROBLEMS

A trained pilot and aeronautical engineer, Broadbent found that many of the problems pilots had, such as misreading dials or pulling the wrong levers, could be solved using psychology. He felt that psychology should be useful, not just theoretical, and his work at the newly founded Applied Psychology Unit at Cambridge pioneered the use of psychology to deal with practical problems.

THE MIND IS AN INFORMATION PROCESSOR

Broadbent believed the mind is a kind of "information processor" that receives, stores, and retrieves the information from our senses. This idea of how our minds work had much in common with the research being done in communications and artificial intelligence after World War II. Always eager to put his theories to practical use, he collaborated with computer scientists on research into human-computer interaction.

STOP THE NOISE

Rather than conducting experiments in the laboratory, Broadbent went into factories and workshops to study the effects of noise, heat, and stress on workers. As a result, he was able to suggest changes in the workplace and in working practices. Improvements of working conditions not only benefited the workers, but also increased their efficiency and productivity.

Watch your

OUR ABILITY TO COMMUNICATE EVEN COMPLEX IDEAS USING SPOKEN AND WRITTEN LANGUAGE IS ONE OF THE THINGS THAT DISTINGUISHES HUMANS FROM OTHER ANIMALS. LANGUAGE ITSELF IS COMPLEX, YET CHILDREN LEARN AT LEAST ONE LANGUAGE EARLY IN LIFE, AND MORE QUICKLY THAN MANY OTHER SKILLS. SO WHAT MAKES LANGUAGE SPECIAL?

See also: 26-27, 42-43

Imitating adults

For a long time, it was thought that we learned language in exactly the same way that we learn other knowledge and skills. Developmental psychologists such as Jean Piaget and Albert Bandura thought that our ability to use language came from

> CHILDREN LEARN **LANGUAGE** BY **IMITATING** OTHERS.
>
> ALBERT BANDURA

imitating our parents and other adults. They suggested that we gradually learn how language works by listening to adults speaking, and then copying what they say. Once we have a grasp of the structures of

language—the grammar—we can use that as a framework and add new words as we pick them up. The behaviorist psychologist B. F. Skinner agreed that we learn language from adults, but also believed that this was a kind of conditioning—a child producing words and sentences is a conditioned response, which is rewarded by smiles and praise from its parents.

Hardwired ability

However, some psychologists felt that language was somehow different from other skills we acquire. As long ago as the 1860s, before psychology had appeared as a science, scientists had discovered that there were specific parts of the brain associated with speech. French physician Paul Broca found that if a certain area of the brain was damaged, this affected a person's ability to produce speech. Following on from Broca's work, German physician and psychiatrist Carl Wernicke identified a different area of the brain associated with understanding speech, and speaking in language that makes sense. These discoveries suggested that some kind of ability to use language is "hardwired" in our brains.

Universal grammar

In the 1960s, the cognitive psychologist and linguist Noam Chomsky came up with a controversial new idea about the way

SIGN SPEAK

A group of deaf children sent to school in Nicaragua developed a unique way to communicate with one another. They had not been taught any sign language, but created a sign language of their own. This evolved into a sophisticated language with a grammar similar to other spoken and written languages, showing that we are born with some fundamental language abilities.

LANGUAGE!

girls usually learn to speak earlier than boys— and the language areas of the female brain are about 17 percent larger.

we learn language. He had noticed that children could understand the meaning of sentences from a very young age, and quickly learned to speak using complex grammatical rules. Nobody had taught them the rules of grammar, yet they appeared to have a grasp of them already. And this was true of children in all cultures, learning and using all kinds of different languages. Chomsky suggested that our ability to learn and use language is something we are born with. We have what he called a "Language Acquisition Device"—a special capacity of our brains that allows us to understand the structure of language. Furthermore, since children everywhere have this same ability to understand grammar, there must be the same underlying structure to all human languages: a "universal grammar." Chomsky's idea of an innate, instinctual capacity for language was very different from previous theories of how we learn language, and not all psychologists agree with him. Some continue to argue that language ability is similar to our other problem-solving capabilities. Canadian cognitive psychologist Steven Pinker, however, supports Chomsky's view, arguing that our capacity for language is inherited, and has come about through evolution.

A CHILD HAS A BUILT-IN ABILITY TO UNDERSTAND GRAMMAR.

THE LANGUAGE ORGAN GROWS LIKE ANY OTHER BODY ORGAN.

NOAM CHOMSKY

Born to talk
Children rapidly learn to construct sentences in a grammatical way without being taught to do so. This suggests that we are born with an understanding of how languages work.

Are you

IT'S DIFFICULT TO GET PEOPLE TO CHANGE THEIR MINDS WHEN THEY HAVE A STRONGLY HELD BELIEF OR OPINION. EVEN WHEN SHOWN EVIDENCE THAT THEY ARE WRONG, THEY INSIST THAT THEY ARE RIGHT. WE ALL DO THIS SOMETIMES, AND EVEN WHEN IT'S OBVIOUS WE ARE MISTAKEN, WE KID OURSELVES THAT WE HAVE GOOD REASON FOR OUR BELIEFS.

Unshakable belief

Our beliefs are very important to us. The way we live our lives is based on the knowledge we have, and what we hold to be true. So when someone questions something we firmly believe, it makes us very uncomfortable. American psychologist Leon Festinger called this feeling of unease "cognitive dissonance." Rather than just accepting that we are wrong, we often become more insistent that we are right. To get rid of the uncomfortable feeling, we justify what we believe and dispute any evidence that contradicts it. Therefore, Festinger realized, it is very difficult to change the mind of someone with strong beliefs: "Tell him you disagree and he turns away. Show him facts or figures and he questions your sources. Appeal to logic and he fails to see your

WORLD TO END ON ~~DECEMBER 21~~ FEBRUARY 20

⟵ Stubborn beliefs

If we believe strongly in something, it's difficult to persuade us that we are wrong, even if there is evidence to suggest it. Rather than change our minds, we tend to believe more strongly, and may even invent further "proof" that we are right.

despite overwhelming evidence that smoking kills, smokers often try to justify their habit.

A MAN WITH CONVICTION IS A HARD MAN TO CHANGE.

LEON FESTINGER

FOOLING yourself?

point." To test his theory, Festinger and his colleagues met members of a cult who claimed to have received messages from aliens predicting the end of the world. When interviewed, the cult members all firmly believed the world was going to end on December 21 of that year. After the apocalypse failed to happen, the psychologists interviewed the members a second time. Rather than give up their story, they declared that the world had been spared because they were such firm believers. To accept that they had been wrong would have caused cognitive dissonance. Instead, their belief had strengthened, and they even claimed to have received another message thanking them for their dedication.

How embarrassing

Festinger noticed that the strongest believers were those who had given up the most for the cult—many had left their jobs and sold their houses. He concluded that the more time and effort someone devotes to something, the more likely they are to defend it. In an experiment, Festinger gave volunteers a series of tedious tasks. He then rewarded some volunteers with one dollar, and others with 20. When asked whether the task had been interesting, the participants who were paid more tended to say no. The poorly paid participants, on the other hand, were more likely to say yes because they needed to justify the amount of effort they had put into the task, for very little reward. In a similar experiment, Eliot Aronson and Judson Mills found that if a task involved some level of embarrassment, this also affected a person's view. They invited female

IF WE DO SOMETHING THAT MAKES US FEEL STUPID, WE FIND A WAY TO JUSTIFY WHAT WE HAVE DONE.
ELIOT ARONSON

students to join a discussion group about the psychology of sex—something the students believed would be fun and interesting. Some students were simply accepted into the group, but others were asked to take an "embarrassment test," in which they had to read aloud a list of obscene words and erotic passages from books—a very humiliating task. All of the participants then heard a recording of a boring discussion about the mating habits of animals, which they were told was the discussion they had volunteered to join. When asked how interesting and enjoyable they had found the talk, the students who had endured the embarrassment test rated it much more favorably than those who had not.

FLORAL FLIGHT

A group of people were asked to try to make a bowl of flowers levitate by concentrating on it. They didn't know that the bowl was equipped with electromagnets, so that it would actually rise off the table. One participant claimed to have seen smoke wisping under the bowl, but another participant, a science teacher, denied that the bowl had risen at all.

How do you make **SENSE** of the world?

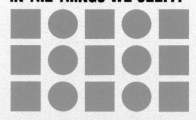

WE TRY TO FIND PATTERNS IN THE THINGS WE SEE...

⬆ Law of similarity
We usually group similar things together, so the picture above is seen as five alternating columns of squares and circles, rather than three rows containing different shapes.

⬆ Law of proximity
We tend to perceive things together if they are close together. We see the picture above as two vertical columns of three spots, and two horizontal rows of three spots.

OUR SENSES, ESPECIALLY SIGHT AND HEARING, GATHER VITAL INFORMATION ABOUT THE WORLD AROUND US. BUT FOR THAT INFORMATION TO BE USEFUL, OUR MINDS NEED TO MAKE SENSE OF IT. THIS MENTAL PROCESS OF ORGANIZING AND INTERPRETING INFORMATION FROM OUR SENSES IS KNOWN AS PERCEPTION.

Recognizing patterns
There is an enormous amount of information in what we see and hear. Our minds examine this incoming information and try to make sense of it and figure out what is important by looking for patterns. For example, when we see a square, our minds don't just see a collection of four lines, but recognize that particular arrangement of lines as a square. In the same way, we recognize the shape of a tune, rather

THE **WHOLE** IS DIFFERENT FROM THE **SUM** OF ITS PARTS.
WOLFGANG KÖHLER

than simply hearing a series of separate notes. A group of early 20th-century psychologists, led by Wolfgang Köhler and Max Wertheimer, were the first to notice how our minds try to see if things have a recognizable form, or "essence"—what they called, in German, a *Gestalt*.

Following the rules
Gestalt psychologists, as they became known, believed that our ability to interpret the information from our senses and recognize patterns is

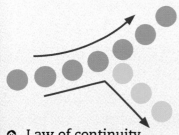

⊕ Law of continuity

Smooth, continuous patterns are more obvious to us than jagged or disjointed ones. Above, we see a smooth upward curve, rather than a line with an angle.

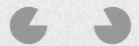

⊕ Law of closure

Our minds supply the missing information in incomplete shapes to separate them from the background. So the picture above can be seen as a triangle on three circles.

THINKING CONSISTS OF UNDERSTANDING STRUCTURES AND PROCEEDING IN ACCORDANCE WITH WHAT WE KNOW.

MAX WERTHEIMER

babies learn to see separate objects by comparing what their eyes see and their hands feel.

"hardwired" into our brains. They argued that our brains organize information in regular ways, looking for particular kinds of patterns. Our perception—the way we interpret sensory information—seems to follow certain rules, which make up the Gestalt Laws of Perceptual Organization. The fact that separate objects can be put together in a certain way to form something different is a key idea in Gestalt psychology, and shows that our initial perception of an overall pattern is different from our perception of its separate parts.

Another dimension

This ability to organize incoming information and find patterns helps us distinguish one thing from another. If we see something and recognize it as a cow

in a field, for instance, we are making a distinction between the figure of the cow and the background. Even when we look at a two-dimensional picture of a cow in a field, we still recognize the difference between figure and background, and use the way the images overlap to determine which objects are near to us and which are farther away. In addition, our minds decipher the patterns of perspective in the picture, and form an idea of the three-dimensional scene it represents—the smaller an object is, the farther away it is. Perspective also helps us identify which direction things are moving in. If something is getting bigger on TV, our minds recognize that it is coming toward us; if it is getting smaller, we assume it's moving away. We interpret the real, three-dimensional world in the same way, using the clues of figure, background, and perspective to determine the relative positions of objects—which is vital for our ability to do practical things.

See also: 78–79

SPOT THE DOG

At first glance, this picture seems to be just a random collection of black splotches on a pale background. But if you are told that it is a picture of a Dalmatian sniffing the ground, you'll probably be able to pick out the pattern of black marks making up the dog from those that form the background.

Don't BELIEVE

OUR PERCEPTION—HOW WE BECOME AWARE OF THINGS THROUGH OUR SENSES—
ALLOWS US TO INTERPRET WHAT WE SEE, HEAR, AND FEEL. THIS HELPS US FIND
OUR WAY AROUND AND DO THINGS IN THE EXTERNAL WORLD, BUT SOMETIMES OUR
MINDS MISINTERPRET THE INFORMATION BECAUSE IT IS AMBIGUOUS OR MISLEADING.
IF OUR PERCEPTION IS WRONG, WE'RE NOT SEEING THE WORLD AS IT REALLY IS.

Seeing things

Gestalt psychologists showed that our
minds look for recognizable patterns
in the information from our senses.
Sometimes, however, our ability to
distinguish patterns lets us down. We
may fail to notice a particular shape
or form, or we may see a pattern
that isn't actually there. Some cognitive
psychologists, including Jerome Bruner
and Roger Shepard, suggested that this
is because, when our minds organize
sensory information, they compare it
to other things we have experienced.
We try to find not just any patterns,
but ones that we know, or those we expect
to be there. Therefore, our minds can
jump to conclusions; they find something
they think they recognize, but they're
mistaken. An example of how shapes
and patterns can mislead our perception
is the fact that people often claim
to see familiar images in odd places—
a face on the surface of Mars, or
Jesus on a piece of toast, for
instance. This also explains
why people sometimes
mistake an unusual cloud
formation for a UFO.

Jumping to conclusions

It's not only that we
misinterpret what our
senses are telling us—
sometimes the actual
information is misleading,
too. The patterns we pick
out give us clues about the
makeup of what we're looking at.

DWARF OR GIANT?

Not all optical illusions are two-dimensional.
In an Ames room, invented by Adelbert
Ames, Jr., two normal-sized people appear
to be completely out of proportion—one
seems to be the size of a dwarf, and the
other a giant. To create the optical illusion,
the walls, ceiling, and floor are slanted, but,
when viewed from a certain angle, the
room appears to be a regular cube.

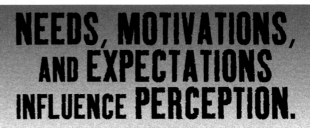

NEEDS, MOTIVATIONS,
AND EXPECTATIONS
INFLUENCE PERCEPTION.

JEROME BRUNER

your EYES

the Ancient greeks didn't know whether optical illusions were a "fault" of the eyes or the mind.

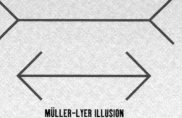
MÜLLER-LYER ILLUSION

← Mind-boggling
Optical illusions such as the Penrose triangle are designed to confuse our senses. And in the Müller-Lyer and Ponzo illusions, the horizontal lines (colored orange in the Ponzo illusion) are the same length.

In a two-dimensional picture, for example, the size of different figures and the way they overlap gives us an idea of which objects are at the front and which are in the distance. Usually, we correctly interpret the clues of perspective—the way that three-dimensional objects are represented in a two-dimensional picture—but sometimes our minds are fooled. Many optical illusions, such as the well-known Ponzo and Müller-Lyer illusions, use tricks of perspective that lead us to reach the wrong conclusion about the size and distance between objects. Others, such as the Penrose impossible triangle, make our minds reel as our perception conflicts with our experience of the world.

PERCEPTION IS EXTERNALLY GUIDED HALLUCINATION.
ROGER SHEPARD

PENROSE TRIANGLE

Direct perception
If our perception of perspective is mistaken, we can make mistakes of judgment when doing things such as trying to catch a ball or turning a corner on a bicycle—and this could be disastrous for someone driving a fast car or flying an airplane. But some psychologists, notably J. J. Gibson, think that we only make this kind of mistake when interpreting two-dimensional images of our three-dimensional world. In the real three-dimensional world, we perceive objects and events directly from our sensory information, without interpreting them by comparing them to our past experiences or what we expect to see. While previous psychologists saw perception as two separate processes—a physical process of perceiving with the senses what something is, and a mental process of perceiving what it means—in Gibson's opinion, it is a single process of direct perception.

PONZO ILLUSION

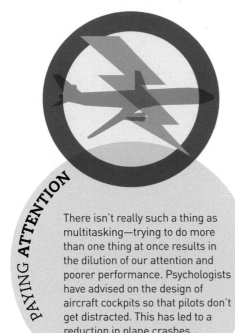

PAYING ATTENTION

There isn't really such a thing as multitasking—trying to do more than one thing at once results in the dilution of our attention and poorer performance. Psychologists have advised on the design of aircraft cockpits so that pilots don't get distracted. This has led to a reduction in plane crashes.

HEADLIGHTS ON

Should people ever turn off their headlights while driving? Research suggests that we should not—even in bright daylight, headlights make a car more visible to others. This has been shown to prevent accidents.

Cognitive psychology in the
REAL WORLD

BACK IN THE ZONE

Cognitive psychologists have found that we are more likely to remember something if we are put back into the environment where we learned it. Based on this theory, patients are taught mobility exercises in hospitals while listening to music, which they can then play at home to remind themselves of the techniques they learned.

SPEED-READING

When you read a piece of text, you don't actually look at every word. This is due to the the way that our minds process information. For example, did you see the repetition of the word *the* in the last sentence? Our brains often pass over mistakes like this, so always remember to proofread your work.

STANDING UP IN COURT

Research suggests that eyewitness accounts can be very unreliable. Cognitive psychologists are often called on to advise on the reliability of witness statements at trials. Their work has even prompted changes to legal systems—in some areas, jurors have to be told about the imperfect nature of memory as a matter of procedure.

RAZZLE-DAZZLE

In World War I, the British and American navies camouflaged warships with complicated geometric patterns, called razzle-dazzle. Rather than trying to hide a ship, these designs were intended to distort the enemy's perception of a vessel's range, direction, size, shape, and speed, and thus reduce losses from torpedo attacks.

Cognitive psychologists study our mental processes, including our attention, memory, perception, and decision-making skills. Understanding these everyday abilities has led to improvements in air and road traffic safety and the justice system, and can even help us remember important information for tests.

Psychological research might even improve your study habits. We remember stuff better if it's broken down into chunks, so divide up your notes under clear headings. We also remember things by visualizing them—so try using doodles and diagrams when you're studying.

RHYME TIME

If you want someone to believe you, speak in rhyme. Psychologists compared rhyming versions of sayings with nonrhyming versions and found that listeners considered the rhyming versions to be more truthful. This is why advertisers often use rhyming slogans to promote products.

STUDY TIPS

What makes me **UNIQUE**?

What makes you so SPECIAL?

What are you LIKE?

So you think you're SMART?

Why are you so MOODY?

What MOTIVATES you?

Do PERSONALITIES change?

Feeling DOWN?

What makes an ADDICT?

What is NORMAL?

Are you INSANE?

Is anyone really EVIL?

It's good to TALK

Is therapy the ANSWER?

Don't worry, be HAPPY!

The psychology of difference, or individual psychology, is concerned with the aspects of our psychological makeup that vary from one person to another. In addition to looking at such things as personality, intelligence, and emotions, this branch of psychology deals with mental disorders and how they can be treated.

What makes you

where you live may determine if nature or nurture plays more of a part in who you are.

WE ALL HAVE DIFFERENT PSYCHOLOGICAL CHARACTERISTICS THAT DETERMINE WHO WE ARE. DIFFERENCES IN PERSONALITY, INTELLIGENCE, ABILITY, AND TALENT ARE WHAT MAKE EACH OF US UNIQUE. BUT WHERE DO THESE TRAITS COME FROM? ARE WE THE PERSON WE ARE FROM BIRTH, OR IS OUR CHARACTER SHAPED BY THE WORLD WE ARE BROUGHT UP IN?

ARE WE SHAPED BY OUR ENVIRONMENT, OR ARE WE BORN THIS WAY?

> **NATURE IS ALL THAT A MAN BRINGS WITH HIMSELF INTO THE WORLD; NURTURE IS EVERY INFLUENCE THAT AFFECTS HIM AFTER HIS BIRTH.**
> FRANCIS GALTON

Nature versus nurture

Long before psychology appeared as a scientific subject, philosophers debated whether humans are born with some existing knowledge of the world, or as "blank slates" who learn everything by experience. Opinion was similarly divided about whether we develop individual characteristics, or are born with them. But in the 19th century, the debate became a question of science, following the publication of Charles Darwin's *The Origin of Species* in 1859, and Gregor Mendel's work on genetic inheritance. These works provided evidence that at least some characteristics—behavioral as well as physical—are inherited. Even so,

⊙ Character growth

Psychologists have argued about whether we grow into who we are as a result of what we are born with, or if our characters are influenced by the world around us. Many believe it is a combination of the two, like a tree that grows naturally but is pruned into shape.

so **SPECIAL?**

many people continued to believe that our environment plays a part in shaping who we are. A cousin of Darwin, Francis Galton, was among the first to examine the scientific evidence, and coined the phrase "nature versus nurture" to describe the two sides of the argument.

> **WITH THE RIGHT NUMBER OF FINGERS AND TOES, EYES, AND A FEW BASIC MOVEMENTS, YOU DO NOT NEED ANY OTHER RAW MATERIALS TO MAKE A MAN, BE THAT MAN A GENIUS, A GENTLEMAN, OR A THUG.**
> JOHN B. WATSON

Are we genetically programmed?

When psychology became a science, the nature versus nurture question divided opinion among psychologists. In the 1920s, two very different views emerged about what gives us our psychological characteristics. On the side of nature, the developmental psychologist Arnold Gesell suggested that humans are genetically programmed to go through patterns of development that determine our characters. We all go through the same series of changes in the same order, and these changes are, in his words, "relatively impervious to environmental influence." In a process he called "maturation," these patterns of change allow our inherited abilities and characteristics to emerge gradually, as we develop physically, emotionally, and psychologically. Taking the nurture point of view, the behaviorist psychologist John B. Watson argued that we do not inherit any psychological traits. In his opinion, our characters, talents, and temperaments are shaped solely by the environment we are brought up in, and especially by the training we are given.

A bit of both

The nature versus nurture debate has continued to the present day, and different approaches to psychology have placed different emphasis on the importance

of heredity and environment. While Darwin's theory of evolution and Mendel's genetics suggested that nature plays the major part, the theories of behaviorism and social psychology in the early 20th century stressed the importance of nurture. Like a pendulum, the argument later swung back to the nature camp with discoveries in modern genetics and biological psychology, and the emergence of the new field of evolutionary psychology inspired by Darwin's theory. Very few psychologists today, however, take standpoints as extreme as those of Gesell or Watson. The generally accepted view is that both nature and nurture play a part in determining human traits, but psychologists may still disagree about exactly how much each factor contributes to our individual characteristics.

See also: 18–19

SEEING DOUBLE

One way to compare the relative importance of nature and nurture is by studying identical twins, especially if they were separated early in life and raised in different families. Identical twins have the same genetic makeup, so any variations in ability, intelligence, and personality are likely to be the result of their different upbringings.

What are you **LIKE?**

WHEN WE TALK ABOUT THE KIND OF PERSON SOMEONE IS, WE USUALLY DESCRIBE THE WAY HE OR SHE THINKS AND BEHAVES. FOR EXAMPLE, SOMEONE MIGHT BE CHEERFUL, RELAXED, AND OUTGOING, OR GLOOMY, ANXIOUS, AND SHY. IT IS THE PARTICULAR COMBINATION OF THESE CHARACTERISTICS THAT MAKES UP OUR UNIQUE PERSONALITIES.

Character traits

A pioneer in the study of personality was Gordon Allport. He noticed that every language has a large number of words to describe aspects of personality—what he called personality "traits." According to Allport, there are two basic kinds of personality traits: common traits, which everybody from the same cultural background has to some degree, and individual traits, which vary from person to person. Each person has a unique combination of these individual traits, and some are more dominant than others. Central traits are the major traits that form our general personalities, but we also have secondary traits, which reveal themselves less consistently in our tastes and preferences, and only in certain situations. In some people, Allport identified a single, or cardinal, trait such as ruthlessness, greed, or ambition, which overshadowed other aspects of their character.

Dim lighting makes people less honest and more likely to cheat, and bright lighting does the opposite.

A MAN CAN BE SAID TO HAVE A TRAIT; BUT HE CANNOT BE SAID TO HAVE A TYPE.

GORDON ALLPORT

Are you an introvert or an extrovert?

By analyzing statistics relating to different personalities, Hans Eysenck developed a theory that focused on types rather than traits. Where Allport had identified an almost infinite number of traits, Eysenck saw these as points on a spectrum of common factors that make up personality (see model of personality, right). He claimed that each personality type could be defined by measuring it on two scales: how shy or outgoing (introverted or extroverted), and how emotionally secure or insecure (stable or neurotic) the person is. He later added a third scale, psychoticism, which measures the kind of characteristics found in people with serious mental disorders. All personality types, Eysenck believed, can be defined by the degree to which they exhibit these three characteristics: extroversion (E), neuroticism (N), and psychoticism (P). Most people's personalities fall between the extremes of these scales, and even a high level of psychoticism, for example, does not imply that a person is psychotic—only that he or she shows some characteristics found in psychotics.

The Big Five

Eysenck's theory of personality types was later modified by other psychologists, including Raymond Cattell, who pointed out that our personalities are not consistent—we behave differently in different situations, and may reveal different aspects of

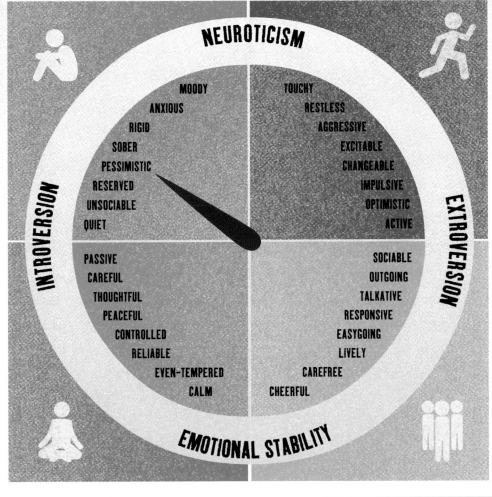

NEUROTICISM

INTROVERSION

MOODY
ANXIOUS
RIGID
SOBER
PESSIMISTIC
RESERVED
UNSOCIABLE
QUIET

TOUCHY
RESTLESS
AGGRESSIVE
EXCITABLE
CHANGEABLE
IMPULSIVE
OPTIMISTIC
ACTIVE

EXTROVERSION

PASSIVE
CAREFUL
THOUGHTFUL
PEACEFUL
CONTROLLED
RELIABLE
EVEN-TEMPERED
CALM

SOCIABLE
OUTGOING
TALKATIVE
RESPONSIVE
EASYGOING
LIVELY
CAREFREE
CHEERFUL

EMOTIONAL STABILITY

⊙ **Four types**
Hans Eysenck's model of personality is based on opposite scales. Each quarter contains traits that may exist in a person of that type—for example, a neurotic introvert might be prone to pessimism.

See also: 88–89, 96–97

our personalities. Others, such as George Kelly, felt that our ideas of our own personalities—how we interpret our observations and experiences—may be different from the way others see us. He called this unique interpretation a "personal construct." In the 1960s, psychologists developed a system of personality types based on five factors (as opposed to Eysenck's three). The types in the "Big Five" model include extroversion and neuroticism, which are much the same as in Eysenck's theory, but psychoticism is replaced by conscientiousness and agreeableness, and there is a new category known as "openness to experience." Most psychologists now accept the Big Five as the most useful and reliable way of categorizing personality types.

FIRST IMPRESSIONS

There may be some truth in the idea that we can "read" people's characters from their faces. We all judge by appearances, and different people can reach very similar conclusions about someone. Recent studies have shown that first impressions can be surprisingly accurate in identifying some personality traits—a withdrawn look, for example, may indicate that a person is an introvert.

GORDON ALLPORT

1897–1967

Often regarded as the founder of personality psychology, Gordon Allport spent most of his working life at Harvard University. He was born in Indiana, the son of a country doctor, and at the age of six moved to Ohio. He first studied philosophy and economics at Harvard, and, after a year in Istanbul, Turkey, returned to earn a PhD in psychology. He also studied in Germany and England, but taught at Harvard from 1924 until his death in 1967.

Allport was shy and solitary at school, and was sometimes teased because he only had eight toes.

A WAY WITH WORDS

Allport was interested in personality very early in his career, and in 1921 he wrote a book with his older brother, Floyd Henry Allport (also a social psychologist), on the idea of personality traits. In later research, Allport and a colleague collected about 18,000 words from dictionaries to describe human characteristics, and organized these into the categories of traits that make up personality.

CHANGING CIRCUMSTANCES

Our personalities are not fixed, according to Allport. Although some traits are consistent, others change over time, and some only show themselves in certain situations. He gave the example of Robinson Crusoe, who only expressed certain traits once he found a companion on his desert island. Allport asked, "Did Robinson Crusoe lack personality traits before the advent of Friday?"

MOTIVE OR DRIVE?

In his work on the reasons for our behavior, Allport made a distinction between what he called motives and drives. The original reason we do something, the motive, can give rise to a drive that is quite separate from it. For example, someone's motive for going into politics may be to improve society and help people, but this may develop into a drive to wield power for its own sake.

"**Personality** is far too complex a thing to be trussed up in a **conceptual straight jacket**."

GOOD VALUES

Allport believed that what people value in life tells us a lot about their personalities. With his colleagues, he conducted a study using multiple choice questions to see how strongly people felt in six basic areas of value: theoretical, their search for truth; economic, what they see as useful; aesthetic, their notions of beauty; social, seeking the love of other people; political, the importance of power; and religious, their need for unity and morality.

So you think you're **SMART**?

INTRAPERSONAL
PEOPLE WHO ARE ABLE TO SELF-REFLECT ARE GOOD AT WRITING AND DRAWING, AND INDEPENDENT ACTIVITIES SUCH AS KEEPING A JOURNAL.

INTERPERSONAL
SOME INDIVIDUALS HAVE A GIFT FOR UNDERSTANDING AND INTERACTING WITH OTHERS AND EXCEL IN GROUP ACTIVITIES.

LOGICAL
AN ABILITY TO REASON, ANALYZE PROBLEMS, AND EXPLORE PATTERNS MAKES SOME PEOPLE GOOD AT SOLVING PUZZLES.

SOME PEOPLE ARE GOOD AT SPORTS, AND OTHERS ARE NOT. SIMILARLY, SOME PEOPLE HAVE BETTER MENTAL ABILITIES. THESE INDIVIDUALS ARE SEEN AS INTELLIGENT, BUT IT'S NOT EASY TO DEFINE EXACTLY WHAT WE MEAN BY INTELLIGENCE, OR TO FIND A WAY OF MEASURING IT. JUST AS THERE ARE MANY KINDS OF PHYSICAL SKILLS, PERHAPS THERE ARE DIFFERENT KINDS OF INTELLIGENCE.

Measuring intelligence

One of the first psychologists to study intelligence, Alfred Binet, was asked by the French government to identify children who would need extra help at school. With his colleague Théodore Simon, he devised a test to measure general mental abilities. It is considered to be the first test to measure intelligence. Since then, numerous different tests have been devised to measure intelligence quotient, or IQ. This is a numerical value reflecting a person's intelligence, which shows how much more or less intelligent he or she is than the average, an IQ of 100. But some psychologists questioned the reliability of these tests. Questions in them reflected the ideas of the test makers as to what defined intelligence—often math and language abilities—and people with abilities in other areas scored low. Tests

KINESTHETIC
OTHER PEOPLE CAN USE THEIR BODIES EFFECTIVELY—THEY ARE SKILLED AT BUILDING THINGS, SPORTS, AND COMMUNICATING WITH BODY LANGUAGE.

LINGUISTIC
OTHER PEOPLE HAVE A WAY WITH WORDS—THEY EXCEL AT READING, WRITING, SPEAKING, PLAYING WORD GAMES, AND GIVING PRESENTATIONS.

MUSICAL
SOME PEOPLE HAVE A GOOD SENSE OF RHYTHM, MELODY, AND HARMONY, AND A TALENT FOR PLAYING MUSICAL INSTRUMENTS.

SPATIAL
PEOPLE SUCH AS ARTISTS AND DESIGNERS HAVE A GOOD AWARENESS OF SPACE AND SHAPES, AND NOTICE FINER DETAILS.

WE JUGGLE DIFFERENT TYPES OF INTELLIGENCE.

were also culturally biased, based on Western ideas of intelligence, and people from other cultures scored badly. Testing and measuring intelligence also gave the impression that intelligence was an unchanging quality, not influenced by environment. This impression was sometimes wrongly used as evidence that some races were genetically less intelligent than others.

From the general to specific

Another question that emerged in intelligence testing was what exactly was being tested. Some people are good at math, others at music or language, but do their skills stem from some kind of general quality that we call intelligence—and if so, how can we test and measure it? In Britain, Charles Spearman found that people who did well on certain types of tests also scored highly on other tests. He developed the idea that there is an innate general intelligence, as well as specific intelligence for specific tasks. Meanwhile, in the United States, psychologists rejected the idea of a single general intelligence. J. P. Guilford argued that intelligence is made up of many different types of mental ability, which could be combined in numerous ways to form up to 150 different types of intelligence. Raymond Cattell, however, accepted Spearman's idea of a general intelligence, but thought that it consisted of both "fluid intelligence" (the ability to solve new problems by reasoning) and "crystallized intelligence" (ability based on knowledge from education and experience).

Multiple intelligences

Later psychologists widened the definition of intelligence even more, moving away from the notion of general intelligence. Robert Sternberg, for example, viewed intelligence as the ability to process

> IF I KNOW YOU'RE VERY **GOOD** IN **MUSIC**, I CAN **PREDICT** WITH JUST ABOUT **ZERO** ACCURACY WHETHER YOU'RE GOING TO BE GOOD OR BAD IN **OTHER THINGS**.
>
> HOWARD GARDNER

information in order to solve problems. He identified three different kinds of problem-solving ability: analytical, the ability to complete the tasks of a traditional intelligence test; creative, the ability to solve new and unusual problems and see things from a different perspective; and practical, the ability to apply skills and knowledge to problems. Howard Gardner developed the idea of different kinds of intelligence further, suggesting that we have "multiple intelligences"—each a separate system of intelligence in a different area of ability. He initially listed seven types of intelligence (see illustration, left). Measuring intelligence in these separate but interacting areas accounts for people's specific abilities, and also helps eliminate the false impression, given by measuring general intelligence, that some cultures or races are more intelligent than others.

> brain size does not correlate with intelligence. Albert Einstein had a lighter brain than the average man.

A HEAD START

In 1968, an experiment in a deprived area of Milwaukee divided 40 newborn babies into two groups. Babies in the first group were given a high-quality preschool education and meals, and their mothers were given child-care and career training. When they started school, these children had higher IQs than the other children, who had received no benefits. But once the benefits stopped, the higher IQs steadily declined, suggesting that intelligence is influenced by our environment.

Why are you so

ANGER   DISGUST   FEAR

OUR EXPERIENCES CAN MAKE US HAPPY, SAD, FRIGHTENED, OR ANGRY. DIFFERENT EMOTIONS AFFECT THE WAY THAT WE THINK, AND CAN EVEN PROMPT A PHYSICAL REACTION. WE HAVE LITTLE CONSCIOUS CONTROL OVER OUR EMOTIONAL REACTIONS, AND OFTEN THEY ARE SO POWERFUL THAT IT'S DIFFICULT TO HIDE THEM OR CONTROL OUR BEHAVIOR.

See also: 46–47, 94–95

Feeling emotional?

Traditionally, it was believed that we learn emotions from the people around us as we grow up, and that emotional responses differ from culture to culture. One of the first to challenge this idea was Charles Darwin, who argued that behavior and physical reactions, such as facial expressions, are associated with the same emotions in all races and cultures. Psychologists later confirmed this theory, but also found that emotions are involuntary—we have no conscious control over them. Dutch psychologist Nico Frijda explained that our emotions are natural reactions that prepare us to deal with life experiences. These involuntary responses are not only felt internally, but also involve spontaneous physical reactions—including laughter, crying, or blushing, as well as facial expressions—which show others our emotions. But Frijda argued that we also have conscious feelings, which come from thinking about our emotions. Unlike emotions, we can control these feelings and hide them from other people.

Overwhelming emotion

Psychologist Paul Ekman traveled widely, studying the physical expressions of emotions in different cultures. He identified six primary emotions: anger, disgust, fear, happiness, sadness, and surprise. Like Frijda, he noticed that these are not conscious, but start before we are

EMOTION IS AN ESSENTIALLY UNCONSCIOUS PROCESS.

NICO FRIJDA

MOODY?

SADNESS   HAPPINESS   SURPRISE

WE ALL HAVE SIX BASIC EMOTIONS.

◉ Masking feelings
Paul Ekman identified six primary emotions, which are common across all cultures. He found that these emotions are so powerful that they are impossible to hide in our faces.

EMOTIONS ARE A RUNAWAY TRAIN.

PAUL EKMAN

aware of them, and are difficult to control. Moreover, they can be so powerful that they override some of our most basic drives. Even if we are hungry, for example, something that provokes disgust can stop us from eating, and sadness can even override our will to live. Ekman also found that it is very difficult to hide emotions. Even if we try to "keep a straight face," telltale signs—microexpressions—can give away our true feelings. These are the "tells" that an experienced poker player looks for in opponents.

What happens first?

While most psychologists agree that emotions are involuntary, there is some debate over how they are connected to our physical reactions, and to our conscious thought and behavior. Common sense tells us that an emotion such as fear comes before physical changes such as sweating, trembling, and increased heart rate, and behavior such as running away. But William James and Carl Lange suggested that it's actually the other way around—if you see something frightening, you sweat and tremble first, and this physical reaction triggers fear. On the other hand, Richard Lazarus argued that some kind of thought process (which may be automatic and unconscious) must appraise the situation before the emotional response, while Robert Zajonc claimed that emotions and thought processes are completely separate, and that emotions may come first.

> women are faster and more accurate at identifying emotions in other people than men.

SMILE AND BE HAPPY

Some psychologists believe that our facial expressions affect how we feel. In one study, participants were asked either to smile or frown while they looked at comic books, but were told they were taking part in an experiment to measure facial muscles. When they were asked about the comics, those who had smiled found them funnier than those who had frowned.

What MOTIVATES

> It takes effort to exercise willpower. That's why we give in to temptation when we're tired.

THERE ARE MANY REASONS WE BEHAVE THE WAY WE DO. OUR ACTIONS HAVE A PURPOSE, AND SOMETHING PROMPTS US TO FULFILL THAT PURPOSE. SOMETIMES OUR NEEDS ARE CLEAR—WE EAT BECAUSE WE ARE HUNGRY— AND SOMETIMES WE DO THINGS FOR THE REWARDS THEY BRING. BUT THE NEEDS AND REWARDS THAT MOTIVATE US ARE NOT ALWAYS OBVIOUS.

See also: 26–27, 102–103

Satisfying your drives

There are many things that we have to do in order to survive, such as breathe, eat, drink, find shelter, and protect ourselves from danger. Looking after our well-being is a fundamental reason for much of our behavior, and we have physiological needs that prompt many of our actions. We experience these as an urge, or "drive," to do things—the drive of hunger, for example, motivates us to find food and eat. According to psychologist Clark Hull, all our behavior is the result of trying to satisfy and reduce the drives of hunger and thirst, the need for rest and activity, and the urge to reproduce. But other psychologists went further, saying that our drives go beyond our physical well-being, and that we actually have other needs that motivate us to do things. For example, we also need to satisfy our need for

WHAT A MAN CAN BE, HE MUST BE.
ABRAHAM MASLOW

psychological health, and our social needs for respect, companionship, and affection from others. This is why psychologists sometimes make a distinction between physical needs and the psychological drives that influence our behavior.

Chasing rewards

While recognizing the effects of these drives on our everyday behavior, some psychologists also pointed out that we are motivated by hedonism—seeking pleasure and avoiding pain. This was a central idea in Sigmund Freud's psychoanalytical theory, but behaviorists, especially B. F. Skinner, also believed that our behavior is motivated by some kind of reward, or avoidance of discomfort. We eat not just to satisfy the drive of hunger, but because we find food enjoyable, and hunger pangs are uncomfortable. The notion of rewards helps explain what motivates us to do things that don't directly impact our physical well-being. While it's true, for example, that children learn through play, learning is not what motivates them—they play because it's fun. Adults, too, do things that

CARROT OR STICK

Offering a reward may not always increase motivation. In one study, some children who enjoyed drawing were given a reward for their pictures. Afterward, those children drew less than the children who had received no reward. They originally drew for enjoyment—a reward from within— rather than for an external reward of money or praise. The reward changed what was enjoyable play into work.

you?

SELF-ACTUALIZATION NEEDS
WHEN WE HAVE MADE FULL USE OF ALL OUR ABILITIES AND FOUND OUR TRUE PURPOSE IN LIFE, WE HAVE ACHIEVED SELF-ACTUALIZATION.

have no apparent, tangible reward, such as hobbies and sports. Some activities—extreme sports or drinking alcohol, for example—might actually harm our physical well-being, but people do them anyway because they enjoy them. And even at work, someone's main motivation might appear to be earning money to pay for food and shelter, but he or she may also enjoy satisfying the drives for achievement, respect, or power.

A hierarchy of needs

Of course, physiological needs such as food, water, and air are more important to us than the psychological need to solve a problem or the social

need for companionship. There are many different kinds of needs, and, according to Abraham Maslow, they can be arranged in order of necessity. Maslow's "hierachy of needs" is often presented as a pyramid diagram, with our basic physical needs at the bottom. Above these are various levels of needs for safety, love, and self-esteem, and at the top are the apparently nonessential needs for self-actualization (achieving our unique full potential) and self-transcendence (doing things for a higher cause than ourselves). To live a fully human life, Maslow believed, we must satisfy the needs on all levels.

ESTEEM NEEDS
WE NEED TO FEEL THAT WE ARE VALUED AND RESPECTED, AND TAKE PRIDE IN OUR ATHLETIC AND ACADEMIC ACHIEVEMENTS.

SOCIAL NEEDS
WE LIKE TO FEEL THAT WE BELONG, AND SEARCH FOR AFFECTION AND ACCEPTANCE AMONG FRIENDS, FAMILY, AND OTHERS.

◉ **Road to fulfillment**
Maslow's original hierarchy included five sets of needs, which can be viewed as essential stages on the road to complete satisfaction.

SAFETY NEEDS
IT'S IMPORTANT FOR US TO FEEL SAFE—SHELTERED FROM THE ELEMENTS AND FREE FROM DANGER AND FEAR.

BASIC NEEDS
HUMANS NEED TO BREATHE, EAT AND DRINK, STAY WARM, REPRODUCE, AND SLEEP IN ORDER TO SURVIVE.

THE ROAD TO SELF-ACTUALIZATION

Do PERSONALITIES

HIS BRANCH LOOKS BETTER THAN MINE...

AND THAT REALLY TICKS ME OFF.

FOUND MY SUNNY SIDE...

FEELING BLUE...

OUR PERSONALITIES ADAPT TO THE SITUATIONS WE ENCOUNTER.

See also: 86–87, 94–95

WHEN WE THINK OF PERSONALITY, WE TEND TO THINK OF WHAT PEOPLE ARE LIKE AND HOW THEY NORMALLY BEHAVE. BUT IS THIS THE SAME AS THE PERSONALITY THEY WERE BORN WITH? DID IT DEVELOP AS THEY GREW UP, AND WILL IT CONTINUE TO CHANGE? OR DO WE HAVE DIFFERENT PERSONALITIES FOR DIFFERENT SITUATIONS?

Developing personality

The two main theories of personality, Hans Eysenck's type theory and Gordon Allport's trait theory, present different ideas about how much of our personality is innate, and how much is determined by our environment. Eysenck's theory implies that personality is mainly genetically determined—something we are born with—and is therefore, to a large extent, fixed and unchanging. On the other hand, Allport's theory acknowledges that personalities change over time and in response to circumstances. Carl Rogers and Abraham Maslow took this further, suggesting that we can modify our personalities in order to fulfill our potential for personal growth. Today, most psychologists believe that both genetics and environment play a part in shaping our personalities, which develop as we go through various stages of our lives such as adolescence and adulthood.

change?

Different situations

These theories may differ in terms of what determines personality, and how much personalities change over time, but they agree that people are predisposed to behave in a certain way, regardless of the situation they are in. American psychologist Walter Mischel challenged this view. He found that personality traits are actually a poor predictor of behavior, and that there is little consistency in the way people behave in different circumstances. He suggested that we look for evidence of a person's personality not in comparatively unchanging traits, but rather in the way he or she behaves in various situations. After all, most of us infer people's personalities

ANY THEORY THAT REGARDS PERSONALITY AS STABLE, FIXED, OR INVARIABLE IS WRONG.
GORDON ALLPORT

only appear in particular situations. As the situations in our lives change, so too does our behavior, revealing different aspects of our personalities. And the traits that show themselves most often and most strongly in our behavior will also change with our circumstances, presenting themselves as a change in personality.

Revealing behavior

Not all psychologists accepted Mischel's overturning of the traditional ideas of personality types and traits in favor of situationism. But he provided good evidence for the idea that there is some interaction between our behavior in different situations and the traits that make up our personalities, and there has been a shift in the study of personality from looking at how personality can be used to predict behavior to how behavior reveals personality.

It takes your brain less than a second to judge a person's attractiveness, competence, and aggressiveness.

BEHAVIOR WITHOUT ENVIRONMENTAL CUES WOULD BE ABSURDLY CHAOTIC.
WALTER MISCHEL

from their actions, rather than from the traits they claim to have. This approach is known as situationism. For example, a man may be considered by everybody (including himself) to have a calm, mild-mannered personality, and when faced with difficult tasks, such as exams, he usually shows these characteristics. When he has to speak in public, however, he becomes very nervous, and when placed in a competitive situation, such as a sports event, he becomes aggressive. All of these traits form part of his personality, but they

THREE-FACED

In a famous case, later made into the movie *The Three Faces of Eve*, a woman displayed two distinct personalities—one neat and prim, the other wild and irresponsible—that seemed to lead separate lives. After treatment, she developed a third personality, which was aware of both of the others and able to balance their extremes.

Feeling DOWN?

AT ONE TIME OR ANOTHER, WE ALL FEEL UNHAPPY. THIS IS USUALLY BECAUSE OF SOMETHING THAT HAS HAPPENED IN OUR LIVES, SUCH AS THE DEATH OF A LOVED ONE OR EVEN JUST A DISAPPOINTMENT, AND WE GET OVER IT IN TIME. SOMETIMES, HOWEVER, THE SADNESS BECOMES OVERWHELMING. BUT IS THERE REALLY A DIFFERENCE BETWEEN UNHAPPINESS AND DEPRESSION?

Sadness and depression

It's completely natural to feel sad when bad things happen to us. But if the sadness is out of proportion to what caused it, and the negative mood continues, we think of it as a disorder called depression. This is caused not so much by external events, but by something inside us, which could be either a neurological or a psychological problem. The boundary between sadness and depression, however, is not clear-cut. Psychologist Aaron Beck devised a multiple-choice questionnaire, the Beck Depression Inventory, which measures a person's degree of unhappiness and negativity by giving a score on a scale running from sadness to serious depression. Psychiatrists also use a set of criteria to determine whether a person has what they call a major depressive disorder, which includes symptoms such as continuous unhappy mood, and loss of interest and pleasure in usual activities.

Stop blaming yourself

Psychiatrists tend to view depression as a disorder involving changes in the brain that can be treated with antidepressant drugs. Psychologists, on the other hand, mostly see the causes of depression as psychological rather than biological. Among the first to take this view was Albert Ellis, who suggested in the mid-20th century that our irrational response to

> **PEOPLE AND THE THINGS WE DO DO NOT UPSET US. RATHER, WE UPSET OURSELVES BY BELIEVING THEY UPSET US.**
> ALBERT ELLIS

See also: 110–111, 112–113

shopping when we're depressed can cause us to spend more money—we buy things to make us feel better.

negative events—rather than the events themselves—can turn our unhappiness into depression. This idea was developed by Aaron Beck, who argued that depression results from an unrealistically negative view of the world. Later, Martin Seligman explained that this attitude was a form of "learned helplessness"—negative events can make us feel that we have no control over what happens to us. He went on to propose that it is how we interpret negative events—for example, by telling ourselves, "I'm stupid," "I always do badly at that kind of thing," or "I get everything wrong"—that brings about despondency and depression. The idea of self-blame also plays a part, according to Australian psychologist Dorothy Rowe, who argued that unhappiness becomes depression when people feel guilty and blame themselves for the bad things that happen in their lives and their resulting misery.

Sadness is normal

A more extreme view of depression is that it is not a disorder at all, but simply a very serious form of unhappiness. Rollo May believed that suffering and sadness are an inevitable part of our lives—part of what it is to be human. Therefore, rather than seeing them as disorders or medical conditions that need to be treated, we should accept our negative feelings as normal and natural. In fact, May argued,

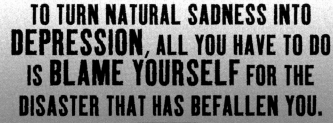

TO TURN NATURAL SADNESS INTO **DEPRESSION**, ALL YOU HAVE TO DO IS **BLAME YOURSELF** FOR THE DISASTER THAT HAS BEFALLEN YOU.

DOROTHY ROWE

they are an essential part of our psychological growth and development. Other psychologists have pointed out that depression is a particular problem in Western society, possibly because of the Western notion that it is normal to be happy. Perhaps this expectation is unrealistic, leading us to feel anxious and guilty about being unhappy, and ultimately resulting in what we call depression.

DON'T GET DEPRESSED...

LOOK ON THE BRIGHT SIDE OF LIFE!

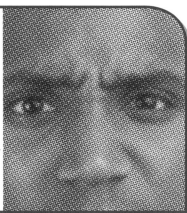

IN TUNE WITH EMOTIONS

Depressed people may have a greater ability to detect emotions. Students at Queen's University in Canada were asked to look at pictures of other people's eyes, and to say if they could tell what emotion the person was feeling. Students who were classified as depressed performed significantly better than those who weren't, and recognized positive as well as negative emotions.

What makes an **ADDICT**?

THERE ARE A LARGE NUMBER OF DRUGS THAT AFFECT HOW OUR BRAIN WORKS. THESE PSYCHOACTIVE DRUGS ARE OFTEN PRESCRIBED BY DOCTORS, BUT MANY ARE ALSO USED RECREATIONALLY—FOR PLEASURE. MOST PEOPLE TAKE DRUGS SUCH AS CAFFEINE FROM TIME TO TIME, BUT SOME BECOME REGULAR USERS AND FIND IT DIFFICULT TO LIVE WITHOUT THEM.

YOU KNOW YOU HAVE A PROBLEM WHEN...

YOU CAN'T FULFILL YOUR OBLIGATIONS AT SCHOOL OR AT WORK: YOU PERFORM BADLY OR DON'T SHOW UP.

YOU USE DRUGS EVEN IN SITUATIONS WHERE YOU'RE PHYSICALLY AT RISK—FOR EXAMPLE, WHEN DRIVING A CAR.

untreated addiction is more expensive than heart disease, diabetes, and cancer combined.

Altering consciousness

Psychoactive, or recreational, drugs are substances that affect our consciousness by changing the way signals are passed around our brains and nervous systems. They can alter our moods and how we perceive things, and these effects are the main reason for most recreational drug use. Different types of psychoactive drugs affect consciousness in different ways. Stimulants, for example, include cocaine and make the user more alert and self-confident. In contrast, depressants, such as alcohol, slow down the mind and body, and create a feeling of calmness. Opiates, including heroin and morphine, also create a feeling of calmness and well-being, while hallucinogenic drugs such as LSD are dramatically mind-altering, distorting normal perception and thought processes.

Substance abuse

Many psychoactive drugs are illegal, but some, such as caffeine, nicotine, and alcohol, are not only legal in most places

ADDICTION IS A STIGMATIZING TERM WHICH IS CULTURALLY CONDITIONED.
THOMAS SZASZ

but also socially acceptable. It is society's attitudes toward certain drugs that influences what we think of as addiction. The psychologist Thomas Szasz pointed out that the word *addict* is often simply a negative label for users of drugs that society disapproves of. It is also loosely used to describe "behavioral addictions" to things such as the Internet or work. Labeling someone as an addict implies that addiction is an illness, and removes responsibility for using the drug from the user. Many psychologists therefore prefer to talk about substance dependence and substance abuse. Substance abuse is

WHEN YOU BLOW YOUR MIND ON DRUGS, YOU REALLY ARE BLOWING YOUR MIND.
SUSAN GREENFIELD

Other drugs do not cause the same kind of physical dependence, but habitual users develop a psychological dependence, requiring more and more of the substance to obtain the pleasurable effect they crave. Early psychological studies tended to view addiction as a kind of illness, but it soon became clear that, in addition to the physical

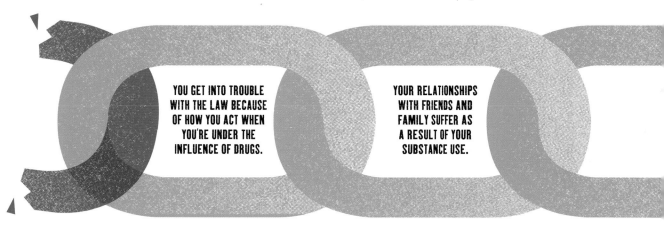

YOU GET INTO TROUBLE WITH THE LAW BECAUSE OF HOW YOU ACT WHEN YOU'RE UNDER THE INFLUENCE OF DRUGS.

YOUR RELATIONSHIPS WITH FRIENDS AND FAMILY SUFFER AS A RESULT OF YOUR SUBSTANCE USE.

difficult to define, but generally, when use of a substance becomes a risk (to the user and others), it is considered abuse— although every drug carries an element of risk, even if it is only taken once.

Dependence

What is often thought of as addiction—not being able to stop using a substance—is known as dependence, which can be physical or psychological. Regular users of some drugs, such as nicotine, become physically dependent on the substance and suffer unpleasant physical withdrawal symptoms when they stop using them— for example, severe headaches or nausea.

effects of psychoactive drugs, social and psychological factors, such as peer group influences and family background, all contribute to substance dependence.

ALTERNATIVE REWARDS

Until recently, it was assumed that people who are dependent on drugs would choose them in preference to food. But a study of heroin-dependent rats has shown otherwise: When offered food at the same time as heroin, the rats chose the food. This suggests that it may be possible to find a substitute reward for even physically dependent drug users.

SIGMUND FREUD

1856–1939

Sigmund Freud was born in Freiberg, Moravia (now part of the Czech Republic), but at the age of four moved with his family to Vienna, Austria, where he spent almost all of his life. He studied medicine and philosophy there, and later developed his technique of psychoanalysis for treating neurotic disorders, including depression and phobias. His work has had a great influence on psychotherapy, even if many of his theories have since been discredited.

HYPNOSIS AND THE "TALKING CURE"

After working as a psychiatrist, Freud studied in Paris with Jean-Martin Charcot, a neurologist who used hypnosis to study hysteria. When Freud returned to Vienna, he set up a private practice with his friend Josef Breuer. They invited patients to talk about their problems while under hypnosis, which, they found, relieved the patients' symptoms. Freud later developed the technique so that patients simply talked freely, without recourse to hypnosis—a process he called psychoanalysis.

TIP OF THE ICEBERG

Freud developed the theory that the conscious mind is like the tip of an iceberg: There is an even bigger unconscious mind that is normally hidden from us, like the part of an iceberg that is concealed underwater. Many psychological problems, he believed, are caused by things that we have repressed but that still lurk in our unconscious, and neurotic disorders can be treated by accessing them through psychoanalysis.

Freud was one of seven children, but he was his mother's favorite. She referred to him as her "golden Siggie."

ANALYSIS OF DREAMS

Freud used various methods to gain access to the thoughts and feelings buried in a patient's unconscious. As he developed his idea of a talking cure, he encouraged patients to talk about whatever came into their minds—a process known as free association. He also asked patients to describe their dreams because he believed that dreams gave an insight into what was going on in the unconscious.

"The **interpretation of dreams** is the royal road to a knowledge of the **unconscious activities** of the mind."

THE FLIGHT FROM NAZISM

Freud traveled widely, lecturing on his theories of psychoanalysis, but he regarded Vienna as his home. When Adolf Hitler came to power in the 1930s, Freud risked persecution from the Nazis due to his Jewish ancestry. Many Jews fled to Britain and the United States at this time, but Freud was reluctant to leave Vienna. In 1938, however, he realized it was unsafe to remain there and fled to London on the Orient Express.

What is **NORMAL?**

EVERY HUMAN IS UNIQUE. IN ADDITION TO PHYSICAL DIFFERENCES, WE EACH HAVE INDIVIDUAL PSYCHOLOGICAL CHARACTERISTICS, SUCH AS PERSONALITY AND INTELLIGENCE, THAT MAKE US RECOGNIZABLY DIFFERENT FROM OTHER PEOPLE. BUT THERE ARE SOME THINGS THAT MOST OF US HAVE IN COMMON—THINGS WE CONSIDER TO BE "NORMAL."

WE TEND TO REJECT THINGS THAT ARE DIFFERENT FROM THE NORM.

See also: 106–107, 112–113

What is abnormal?

We may have a good idea of what we consider to be normal, but it's not easy to define exactly what we mean by normality. Behavior that is considered normal in one culture may be deemed strange in another, and we each have our own ideas of what is normal. One way of trying to define *normal* is to look at what we consider to be abnormal. This could be simply behavior that is different from how most people behave—yet the word *abnormal* also suggests that something is undesirable or unacceptable. People with special talents, for example, are not seen as abnormal, but exceptional. When we label people as abnormal, we are saying that they are not as we think they should be. Just as we have an idea of physical health, we measure people by an idea of normal mental health, and tend to describe those who deviate from this as having a mental disorder or illness. And because we see those people as different, there is often a stigma attached to mental disorders.

> IT IS A PHYSICIAN'S **DUTY** TO UNDERSTAND THE **NATURE** OF **INSANITY.**
>
> EMIL KRAEPELIN

Classifying mental disorders

In medieval times, abnormal behavior was thought to be caused by witchcraft, but, as science progressed, attitudes changed, and it became regarded more as a type of disease. Psychiatry emerged in the 19th century as a branch of medicine

Finding fault

We recognize normality in many aspects of day-to-day life, and tend to avoid things that we consider "abnormal." Even when buying carrots, we naturally prefer the more carrotlike ones.

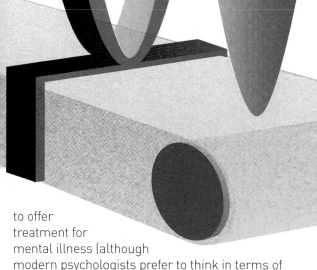

> # IN THE PAST, MEN CREATED WITCHES: NOW THEY CREATE MENTAL PATIENTS.
> **THOMAS SZASZ**

brain that were incurable. His classification was the first of its kind, and formed the basis for modern systems of classifying various mental disorders, such as the World Health Organization's International Classification of Diseases (ICD), and the American Psychiatric Association's Diagnostic and Statistical Manual of Mental Disorders (DSM). Both list disorders stemming from brain disease or damage, schizophrenia, substance abuse disorders, mood disorders, anxiety disorders, personality and behavioral disorders, and eating and sleeping disorders.

Problems in living

Not all psychologists agree with labeling so-called "abnormal" behaviors as medical conditions that require treatment. One critic of this practice was Thomas Szasz, who believed that unless there is a physical cause such as brain damage, mental disorders should be considered not as illnesses, but as "problems in living" resulting from things that ordinary people have to deal with in everyday life, such as the end of a relationship or the death of a relative. In his view, many of the conditions psychiatrists describe as mental disorders, including depression and anxiety, are in fact a normal part of human life. Although this is an extreme view, most psychiatrists and psychologists recognize that there is a difference between organic mental disorders (those with a physical cause) and functional disorders (those that Szasz has described as "problems in living").

to offer treatment for mental illness (although modern psychologists prefer to think in terms of mental disorders, rather than illness). One of the pioneers of psychiatry, Emil Kraepelin, believed that mental illness had physical causes, like any other disease. He identified two types of mental illness: manic-depressive psychosis (now known as mood or affective disorder), caused by external conditions and therefore curable; and dementia praecox (now called schizophrenia), caused by physical problems in the

> **In the Middle Ages, people who behaved in an unusual way were thought to be possessed by demons.**

Are you INSANE?

THE TERM *INSANITY* HAS OFTEN BEEN USED TO DESCRIBE BEHAVIOR THAT WE CONSIDER "CRAZY." TODAY, THIS LABEL IS SEEN NOT ONLY AS UNHELPFUL AND STIGMATIZING, BUT UNSCIENTIFIC. WHAT WAS TRADITIONALLY THOUGHT OF AS INSANITY IS NOW CLASSIFIED AS DIFFERENT MENTAL DISORDERS, OR RECOGNIZED AS UNPREDICTABLE BEHAVIOR.

Madness or illness?

For much of human history, people exhibiting extremely abnormal behavior were labeled as "insane" or "mad," and seen as somehow different from "normal" people. In the 19th century, however, attitudes changed, and the new science of psychiatry began to regard this "insane" behavior as a sign of mental illness or disease. Psychiatrists also recognized that there was not just one kind of "madness," but a variety of mental disorders with different symptoms and varying degrees of severity. Unpredictable or unexpected behavior began to be classified as psychosis, an abnormality of the mind, which in its severest form is now known as schizophrenia. Early psychiatrists believed that this disorder was caused by physical problems in the brain and was an incurable illness with

⊘ Living on the edge
We all do things that other people might regard as crazy. But people who enjoy skydiving, for instance, are not crazy—they're simply doing something that's different from the norm.

PEOPLE WHO DO CRAZY THINGS AREN'T NECESSARILY CRAZY.

SOME **SITUATIONS** CAN MOVE A GREAT PROPORTION OF US **"NORMAL"** ADULTS TO **BEHAVE** IN VERY **UNAPPETIZING** WAYS.

ELLIOT ARONSON

recognizable symptoms, such as paranoia, hallucinations, delusions, and confused behavior and speech.

Crazy behavior

Of course, not all abnormal behavior is caused by schizophrenia. There is a range of other mental conditions, including mood disorders such as depression, personality disorders, as well as anxiety disorders and phobias. Recognition of these different mental disorders encouraged a change of perspective: People previously regarded as insane were now seen to be suffering from some kind of "insanity." Elliot Aronson took this shift of perspective a step further, arguing that people who do crazy things aren't necessarily crazy. What seems to be abnormal behavior, he said, is often not caused by any kind of mental disorder, but by circumstances that make us react in ways that diverge from the norm. When faced with an extreme situation, such as a tragic accident or crime, it is common to behave in a way that appears insane. Therefore, before labeling somebody as "mad," "insane," or "psychotic," Aronson said that it is important to understand the reasons for his or her behavior.

There's no such thing as "crazy"

Aronson showed that strange behavior is not always evidence of a mental disorder, but some psychologists went further, controversially rejecting the idea of mental illness altogether. Thomas Szasz suggested that unless there is a physical cause, such as brain disease, mental disorders are simply disproportionate reactions to everyday issues such as the death of a loved one.

> In the 18th century, cold bathing was believed to cure insanity as well as intoxication.

SOCIETY HIGHLY VALUES ITS NORMAL MAN... NORMAL MEN HAVE KILLED PERHAPS 100,000,000 OF THEIR FELLOW NORMAL MEN IN THE LAST 50 YEARS.

R. D. LAiNG

Some even argued that mental disorders should not be seen as medical conditions requiring medical treatment. At the forefront of this "antipsychiatry movement" was R. D. Laing, who felt that even conditions like schizophrenia were not illnesses, but ways for society to label people whose behavior does not fit in with social norms. For Laing, there is no such thing as a mental illness, nor can we make a distinction between insanity and sanity. While this is an extreme view, Laing has influenced psychologists such as Richard Bentall, who suggests that the line between mental illness and health is not clear-cut, and that even some forms of schizophrenia should be considered psychological disorders rather than purely physiological illnesses.

See also: 104–105, 112–113

CRAZILY HAPPY

In 1992, Richard Bentall said that happiness should be considered a psychiatric disorder. Although his suggestion was tongue-in-cheek, it had a serious message. It is statistically abnormal to be happy, and happiness causes recognizable symptoms of abnormal behavior— such as a carefree attitude and impulsive behavior—just like other mental disorders.

Is anyone really

WE ALL OCCASIONALLY DO THINGS THAT WE KNOW ARE WRONG, BUT CERTAIN PEOPLE ARE MORE LIKELY TO COMMIT CRIMES THAN OTHERS. SOME ARE HABITUAL PETTY CRIMINALS, AND OTHERS REGULARLY COMMIT CRUEL AND VIOLENT ACTS. THESE ACTIONS ARE OFTEN DESCRIBED AS "EVIL," AND THE OFFENDERS ARE LABELED AS EVIL PEOPLE, OR PSYCHOPATHS.

> **PSYCHOPATHS** SHOW A STUNNING **LACK** OF **CONCERN** FOR THE **EFFECTS** THEIR ACTIONS HAVE ON OTHERS, NO MATTER HOW **DEVASTATING** THESE MIGHT BE.
>
> **ROBERT D. HARE**

See also: 112–113, 122–123

Evil actions

What actions make a person "evil"? Society decides what it considers "bad" behavior, and calls these actions crimes, but these include minor crimes such as shoplifting, which we don't normally consider to be evil. What we think of as evil acts are generally the most serious crimes, including murder, rape, and assault. But is it right to label such offenders as evil? Good people may cause harm in extreme circumstances—killing in self-defense, for example. But some people regularly commit cruel and violent crimes. Rather than simply labeling them as evil, however, some psychologists have asked whether these individuals choose to do evil things, or whether they have an innate personality type, or an abnormality or illness, which causes them to engage in criminal behavior.

A guilty conscience makes us want to get physically clean—this is known as the Lady Macbeth effect.

Personality disorder

By analyzing crime statistics, such as the age, gender, intelligence, and social background of offenders, psychologists have tried to determine what factors are involved in habitual criminal behavior, especially in serious crimes. Although social background plays a part, many believe that personality is more important. Robert D. Hare suggested that violent, criminal behavior results from a personality disorder, sometimes known as psychopathy, but which he called antisocial personality disorder (APD). He found a number of personality traits that are characteristic of APD, and devised his Psychopathy Checklist for identifying the disorder. The checklist is divided into two main categories. The first identifies traits

CRIMINAL PROFILING

A new branch of psychology, investigative psychology, now provides information that can be used by the police. An important part of investigative psychology is criminal profiling, using evidence from a crime scene to get an idea of the criminal's personality and motivation, in order to narrow down the range of potential suspects.

EVIL?

Dark side ➔

Some psychologists believe that people who commit evil acts have a built-in personality disorder, called psychopathy. Psychopaths have a lack of empathy, and thus don't mind hurting others.

DO YOU HAVE AN EVIL STREAK?

such as selfishness, deceit, and a callous lack of remorse or guilt, while the second identifies elements of an unstable, antisocial lifestyle, including an exploitative dependence on others. Recent research has shown some correlation between APD and certain types of brain abnormalities, but the link has not been proven, and environmental factors are also associated with the development of the disorder.

Treatment and punishment

Society largely deals with criminals by punishing them, usually by putting them in prison. Offenders may also receive psychological treatment to deter them from committing future crimes. While these methods can be successful with some people, those with APD are largely undeterred by prison or techniques such as psychotherapy. Treatment of APD is controversial, and some psychologists believe that identifying somebody as a psychopath is not helpful. Hare's checklist has also been criticized because some individuals scoring highly may be merely irresponsible, impulsive, or emotionally detached, but are not necessarily serious criminals. And others who have a form of APD do not commit crimes, but exhibit the disorder by becoming bullying bosses, or even tyrannical dictators or military leaders.

It's good to TALK

THROUGHOUT HISTORY, PEOPLE HAVE LOOKED FOR WAYS OF DEALING WITH DISTRESSING PROBLEMS SUCH AS ANXIETY AND DEPRESSION. THESE WERE NOT RECOGNIZED AS MENTAL DISORDERS UNTIL THE 19TH CENTURY, WHEN PSYCHOTHERAPY EVOLVED FROM THE IDEA THAT UNDERSTANDING THE CAUSES OF THESE DISORDERS WOULD HELP RELIEVE THEM.

> A MAN SHOULD NOT STRIVE TO ELIMINATE HIS **COMPLEXES**, BUT TO GET INTO **ACCORD** WITH THEM.
>
> SIGMUND FREUD

See also: 102–103

A talking cure

The pioneer of treating mental disorders by finding out what caused them was Sigmund Freud. He had worked with a neurologist, Jean-Martin Charcot, who used hypnotism to treat patients with "hysteria." These were mostly women showing extreme signs of distress. Freud went on to work with physician Josef Breuer, who hypnotized his patients and then asked them to talk about their symptoms. One case in particular was striking—that of a woman referred to as Anna O. Breuer found that as Anna recalled memories of traumatic events from her past, her condition improved. This "talking cure," as she called it, led the two men to believe that the symptoms of anxiety and depression—neurotic behavior— could be relieved by allowing patients to talk freely about their ideas, memories, and dreams. Freud then developed a theory that we often try to forget unpleasant or traumatic memories, but that they're not actually forgotten. Instead, they are repressed— pushed deep into our unconscious minds.

He also suggested that there is a conflict in our minds between what we consciously think (the part of the mind he called the ego), our instinctive drives or physical needs (the unconscious part of the mind he called the id), and our inner "conscience," or what we have been told is right and wrong (the part of our unconscious he called the superego).

Psychoanalysis

Freud believed that analyzing the repressed memories and conflicts in the unconscious gave patients insight into their mental problems, so that they could then overcome them. This technique, known as "psychoanalysis," soon became a popular

Sigmund Freud's youngest daughter, Anna, was also a famous psychoanalyst, who expanded on his theories of the unconscious.

Freeing the unconscious ⬆

Freud believed that talking was the best cure for mental disorders. By revealing their hidden thoughts and dreams to a therapist, patients could release repressed memories and relieve their distress.

treatment for disorders such as anxiety and depression. Colleagues embraced Freud's approach, and introduced new ideas to his theory of the unconscious. Alfred Adler, for example, emphasized the effects of feelings of inferiority (what he called an "inferiority complex") on a person's mental health, while Carl Jung focused on the interpretation of dreams and symbols, and proposed that, in addition to our personal unconscious mind, there is a "collective unconscious" of ideas common to all of us.

TRUTH CAN BE TOLERATED ONLY IF YOU UNCOVER IT YOURSELF.
FRITZ PERLS

Making life changes

Many psychotherapists adopted Freud's methods, but not all of them agreed with his theories of the unconscious. Some considered the

developed in the 1940s and 1950s by Fritz and Laura Perls, and Paul Goodman. Gestalt therapy placed more emphasis on the present than the past, and on establishing a relationship with a therapist in order to discuss ways of making life changes. Although modern psychotherapy has developed into something very different from Freud's psychoanalysis, the basic idea of dealing with problems by talking about them continues to develop alongside other treatments for many common mental disorders.

TALKING SETS UNCONSCIOUS THOUGHTS FREE...

theories to be unscientific— based on speculation rather than hard evidence—and Hans Eysenck questioned whether psychoanalysis was ever effective. Others, while disagreeing with Freud, believed in the benefits of some form of talking cure, but felt that it was more helpful to let patients talk about all aspects of their lives, rather than trying to analyze their unconscious. One such alternative form of psychotherapy, Gestalt therapy, was

SLIP OF THE TONGUE

It's difficult to hide what's repressed in our unconscious completely, and sometimes the thing that's troubling us reveals itself without our realizing it. When we're talking, we might show our true feelings in our body language. Or we might use the wrong word for something—a mistake known as a Freudian slip—revealing what is really on our minds.

Is therapy the ANSWER?

IN ADDITION TO TRYING TO UNDERSTAND OUR MINDS AND BEHAVIOR, PSYCHOLOGY IS CONCERNED WITH FINDING WAYS OF TREATING MENTAL DISORDERS. CLINICAL PSYCHOLOGY, THE BRANCH OF PSYCHOLOGY THAT EXAMINES MENTAL HEALTH, INCLUDES MANY DIFFERENT KINDS OF TREATMENT, WHICH ARE GENERALLY KNOWN AS PSYCHOTHERAPY.

> **IF A PROBLEM IS OVERWHELMING, BREAK IT DOWN INTO MANAGEABLE PIECES.**

A spoonful of medicine

Mental disorders were considered to be incurable illnesses until a branch of medicine, psychiatry, emerged to try to find treatments for them. Advances in neuroscience have improved our knowledge of the brain and nervous system, and doctors have developed a range of different treatments that change the way our brains work. These include surgery, which involves physically removing or isolating parts of the brain; electroconvulsive therapy (ECT), in which an electric current is passed through the brain; and drugs, which alter the chemical connections in the brain. These methods have been used to treat disorders that have an obvious physical cause, such as brain damage, but doctors have also found that they relieve the symptoms of other mental disorders. Surgery and ECT are now considered very invasive treatments, and are only used in cases where other treatments have failed, but drugs such as antidepressants and antipsychotics are regularly used for a number of mental disorders. Modern psychiatry, however, does not rely only on these physical treatments, and most patients receive a combination of medication and psychotherapy.

> **I CONCLUDED THAT PSYCHOANALYSIS WAS A FAITH-BASED THERAPY.**
> **AARON BECK**

Psychological approach

Psychotherapy developed from the idea that not all mental disorders are physical, medical illnesses. In fact, they are psychological problems, and thus require some form of psychological treatment. Sigmund Freud pioneered the use of therapy to treat what he called neurosis, which included disorders such as anxiety and depression that are not caused by brain damage or disease. Psychoanalysis, based on Freud's theories of the unconscious mind, was a common alternative treatment for such disorders until psychologists began to question its effectiveness. One such psychologist was Joseph Wolpe, who found that

In traditional "lunatic" asylums, mentally ill patients endured terrible conditions.

psychoanalysis offered little relief to soldiers suffering from post-traumatic stress disorder. Inspired by the behaviorist idea of conditioning—learning a particular response to a stimulus—Wolpe created behavior therapy, which focused on changing patients' responses. The therapist plays a more active role in behavior therapy, using techniques such as systematic desensitization (gradually exposing the patient to the things that cause fear and anxiety, in relaxing conditions) and aversion therapy (conditioning the patient to associate undesirable behavior with something unpleasant). Wolpe argued that if patients' behavior could be changed, their negative thoughts and feelings would diminish.

Banishing negative thoughts

Other psychologists felt that behavior therapy was not the answer either. Influenced by cognitive psychology— the study of how the mind works— they suggested that if the negative thoughts and feelings were treated,

the behavior would then correct itself. Aaron Beck, a psychotherapist who had become disillusioned with psychoanalysis, developed a cognitive therapy that helped patients find ways of thinking differently about their problems, and overcome their tendency to see only the negative side of things. Beck encouraged his patients to examine their thoughts and feelings, instead of being victims of negative "automatic thoughts." Meanwhile, Albert Ellis was developing a similar form of cognitive therapy, Rational Emotive Behavior Therapy, which urged patients to think rationally in the face of difficulty, rather than to allow irrational negative thoughts to overwhelm them. Both Ellis and Beck went on to combine cognitive and behaviorist ideas to develop cognitive behavioral therapy (CBT), which has proved effective in treating many different mental disorders. CBT works on the theory that problems are caused not by situations, but by how we interpret those situations in our thoughts, and how we feel and act as a result of this interpretation.

Trepanning was first used for mental illness in the stone age. A hole was drilled in the patient's head to release evil spirits.

See also: 98–99, 110–111

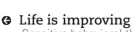

⊖ Life is improving
Cognitive behavioral therapy deals with current issues, rather than delving into a patient's past. By examining and breaking them down into smaller pieces, patients are able to manage their problems in a more positive way.

VIRTUAL REALITY
Cognitive behavioral therapy has been particularly successful in treating people with phobias, such as the fear of spiders or flying. When it was first used, therapists got their patients to think differently about the thing they were afraid of, and gradually exposed them to it. Modern computer technology allows phobics to experience the object of their fears in virtual reality before being exposed to it in real life.

Don't worry, be

MUCH OF THE STUDY OF PSYCHOLOGICAL DIFFERENCES HAS CONCENTRATED ON ABNORMALITIES AND MENTAL DISORDERS. BUT A NUMBER OF PSYCHOLOGISTS IN THE LATE 20TH CENTURY OPTED FOR A MORE POSITIVE APPROACH, LOOKING AT HOW WE CAN LEAD HAPPY AND FULFILLING LIVES.

FIND YOUR FLOW OF HAPPINESS.

The good life

The move away from the negative side of our psychological makeup came, at first, from the world of psychotherapy. Some psychotherapists, using Sigmund Freud's methods of psychoanalysis, began to question if it was helpful to concentrate on mental disorders that required treatment. Instead, they suggested focusing on mental health, and ways of achieving it. Abraham Maslow, one of the first to take this new perspective, thought that we should stop looking at people as "a bag of symptoms" and consider their positive qualities, too. Similarly, Erich Fromm believed that many mental problems can be overcome by discovering our own individual ideas and abilities and finding fulfillment in our lives. Another influential psychotherapist taking this approach was

> Happiness takes effort. Don't just avoid doing unpleasant tasks— you also need to actively do pleasant ones.

See also: 98–99, 112–113

Carl Rogers, who thought that any therapy should be centered on the individual, helping him or her live what he called "the good life," in which a person is not only happy, but also fulfilled. Mental health, in his opinion, is not a fixed state, but something we can achieve through a process of discovery and growth, by taking responsibility for who we are and living life to its fullest.

The search for happiness

This shift in emphasis from treating mental disorders to helping people live a "good life" inspired a movement that became known as "positive psychology." At the forefront of this approach is Martin

> **THE PROCESS OF THE GOOD LIFE...
> MEANS LAUNCHING ONESELF FULLY
> INTO THE STREAM OF LIFE.**
> CARL ROGERS

HAPPY!

⊘ In your own world
Musicians can be so deeply absorbed in their music that they cut themselves off from the world around them, achieving an intense feeling of happiness.

Seligman. In order to live a happy life, he says, we have to know what will make us happy. By analyzing the lives of happy and fulfilled people, he identified three essential elements. One is what he calls "the pleasant life"—the kind of pleasure-seeking and socializing we generally associate with being happy. But although this is an important part of a happy life, it does not lead to lasting happiness. For that, we must also derive reward and fulfillment from what, like Rogers, he calls "the good life"—achieving personal growth by doing things we want to do, as well as we can—and "the meaningful life," doing things not for ourselves but for other people or for a greater cause.

Rewarding work

The Hungarian-born psychologist Mihály Csíkszentmihályi also studied people who felt they led happy and fulfilling lives. He found that although they derived satisfaction from many different things, they all described a similar feeling when they were totally absorbed in what they were doing. It was a sensation of timelessness, when they felt calm, focused, and unaware of themselves or

> # ECSTASY IS A STEP INTO AN ALTERNATIVE REALITY.
> ### MiHÁLY CSÍKSZENTMiHÁLYi

the world around them. This state of "flow," as Csíkszentmihályi called it, is similar to the trancelike state a musician experiences when playing an instrument. We can achieve flow in any task, not only creative activities such as music or art, as long as it is not beyond our capabilities, yet still offers a challenge. And the feeling of intense pleasure it creates can make not only our leisure pursuits, but also our work, rewarding and meaningful.

FEEL-GOOD DEEDS

A 2005 study showed that being kind to others increases our well-being. Students were asked to perform five acts of kindness every week for six weeks, either doing one act each day or all five acts on one day. Students who did one daily act of kindness showed a slight increase in well-being, but those who did all five in one day improved their well-being by as much as 40 percent.

FEELING BRIGHT

Psychological studies have shown that both sunlight and artificial light can reduce the symptoms of seasonal affective disorder (SAD), which include tiredness, stress, and general unhappiness. SAD is thought to result from reduced exposure to sunlight during the winter months.

GUILTY FACES

The small, unconscious variations in our facial expressions, often called "microexpressions," can reveal our underlying emotions. Experts look for these in order to tell if a person is lying—for example, security agencies use them to try to pick out terrorists.

Psychology of difference in the
REAL WORLD

BEATING THE BLUES

Studies show that the effects of antidepressant drugs can be improved when combined with regular exercise. Physical activity releases endorphins—the body's natural antidepressants. Exercise is also a healthy way to rid your mind of worries—in contrast to unhealthy habits, such as drinking.

AN OPEN MIND

Psychologists have found that being open-minded naturally increases good fortune. People who are willing to be flexible and embrace opportunities in life, love, and work—even if these involve some kind of risk—generally feel more fulfilled and positive than more cautious types.

Personality tests formulated by psychologists can be useful in helping students choose careers that suit them. These tests are also used in conjunction with interviews, helping employers select candidates whose personalities will be compatible with the work required.

A GOOD MATCH

YOU NEED THIS

Advertisers try to sell us products by associating them with basic human needs such as love and safety. For example, advertisements for perfume often suggest that it will make you more attractive to the opposite sex, and insurance companies emphasize that their policies protect your family.

We all have very different personalities and abilities, and some people suffer from psychological disorders, such as depression and schizophrenia. By understanding these individual differences, psychologists can help treat people's problems, and encourage us all to live happy and fulfilling lives.

ARRAY OF TALENTS

Contrary to popular belief, psychologists have found that there are multiple types of intelligence. Some people are bad at tests but show remarkable abilities elsewhere. For example, bookies often leave school early, yet are able to perform complicated calculations in their heads.

BREAKING BAD HABITS

Why are some people addicted to smoking? Research has shown that although people often want to stop, they find themselves continuing to smoke because they associate certain situations, such as socializing or stress, with their habit. If they change the situation, it is easier to quit smoking.

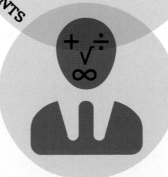

Where do I FIT IN?

Would you follow the CROWD?

Why do GOOD people do BAD things?

Don't be so SELFISH!

ATTITUDE problem?

The power of PERSUASION

What makes you ANGRY?

Are you in the IN CROWD?

What makes a WINNING TEAM?

Can you PERFORM under PRESSURE?

Do GUYS think like GIRLS?

Why do people fall in LOVE?

Social psychology examines the way we interact with other people, how we behave as part of a group, and what effects other people have on us. In addition to how we get along with others at work, at play, and in our personal lives, it includes the study of how our attitudes and behavior are shaped by society.

Would you follow

OUR BEHAVIOR IS GREATLY INFLUENCED BY THE PEOPLE AROUND US. WE BELONG TO DIFFERENT SOCIAL GROUPS, SUCH AS OUR FRIENDS AND FAMILY, AS WELL AS BEING PART OF WIDER SOCIETY. ALTHOUGH WE LIKE TO BELIEVE THAT WE ARE INDEPENDENT INDIVIDUALS, WE MAY FEEL PRESSURE TO CONFORM TO THE OPINIONS OF THESE GROUPS.

> A MEMBER OF A TRIBE OF CANNIBALS **ACCEPTS** CANNIBALISM AS ALTOGETHER **FITTING** AND **PROPER.**
>
> SOLOMON ASCH

A need to conform

An important goal of social psychology is to examine how our thoughts and behavior are affected by our social groups. A number of studies have demonstrated our natural desire to conform to what a group as a whole thinks. One of the first of these experiments was carried out in 1932 by A. Jenness, who asked individual students to guess how many beans were in a bottle. The students were then told to discuss the question together, before giving

their individual answers again. Jenness found that all of the participants adjusted their original guess to be closer to the group's estimate. Taking a different approach, Solomon Asch placed some unwitting subjects individually into groups of his accomplices (who were introduced as fellow participants). When asked several questions about the length of lines in a picture, the accomplices gave answers that were at first right and then blatantly wrong. Even when the answers were obviously incorrect, the unwitting participants went along with the majority opinion for about a third of the time, and three-quarters of them gave at least one wrong answer.

Under pressure

Interviewed after the experiment, Asch's unwitting participants all said that they had felt self-conscious and anxious during

> conformity can have a positive effect— evidence shows that smokers tend to quit in clusters.

Toe the line ❷

In Asch's experiment, participants were asked which line—A, B, or C—was the same length as the line on the left of the card. Many people just gave the same answer as everyone else, even though they knew it was wrong.

the CROWD?

the experiment, and feared not being approved of by the group. Most reported that they disagreed with the others; some went along with the majority even though they knew it was wrong, rather than make themselves conspicuous; and a few said that they had come to believe that the group was correct. With this and similar experiments, psychologists have shown that we feel pressure to conform when in a group. We need the acceptance and approval of others, and even when we disagree with them, we are prepared to comply in order to fit in. But we also have a need to feel certain about our opinions, and look to others for confirmation or guidance, which can lead us to doubt ourselves and change our views.

Sticking to your beliefs

Not everyone is prepared to give in to the real or imagined pressure to conform, however. In Asch's experiments, there were many who did not conform, and in similar studies, when people were asked to write down their answers or give them in private, there were many more who stood by their opinions. And if one of the accomplices also disagreed with the

CHAIN REACTION

The dynamics of crowd applause also suggest our need to conform. Scientists in Sweden have found that it takes only one or two individuals to start a round of applause, or to stop it, as people feel a social pressure to follow others. This tendency to join a trend also explains why people follow popular stories or join groups on Facebook and Twitter.

wrong answers, even fewer of the participants conformed. The Asch experiment has been replicated in various parts of the world, and results suggest that conformity varies across different cultures. In the collectivist societies of Asia and Africa, where the needs of the group are put before those of the individual, more participants conformed than in studies carried out in the individualistic West, where personal choice is more highly valued.

WHICH LINE IS THE SAME AS THE FIRST LINE?

A B C

Why do **GOOD** people

HUMANS ARE CAPABLE OF TERRIBLE VIOLENCE AND CRUELTY—EVEN ORDINARY PEOPLE WHO LEAD OTHERWISE GOOD LIVES. THEY DEFEND THEIR ACTIONS BY BLAMING CIRCUMSTANCES, OR CLAIM THEY WERE SIMPLY FOLLOWING ORDERS. PSYCHOLOGISTS HAVE SOUGHT TO DISCOVER HOW PEOPLE COME TO DO THESE THINGS.

A shocking experiment

After the atrocities committed by the Nazis in World War II, psychologists began to question if only certain kinds of people were capable of doing such horrific things, or if, in similar circumstances, most of us would do the same. Two famous (and controversial) experiments came to some uncomfortable conclusions. In the first, Stanley Milgram examined how much we will obey authority. He recruited men to take part in a study about learning, offering every applicant $4.50. Each participant was introduced to Mr. Wallace, who was pretending to be another participant with a heart condition. They drew lots to see who would be the "teacher" and the "learner" (the process was rigged so the real participant was always the teacher), and went into adjoining rooms. The teacher then had to ask Mr. Wallace, the learner, a series of questions, and was instructed by a "supervisor" to give the learner an electric shock of increasing voltage for every wrong answer (in fact, there was no electric shock). If the teacher hesitated, the supervisor told him to continue. The first shocks made Mr. Wallace grunt with pain. As the voltage got higher, he began to complain, then shouted in protest, and at 315 volts he screamed violently. Above 330 volts, there was silence.

we are more likely to obey an authority figure if he or she is wearing uniform—especially a police uniform.

Under orders

Milgram found that all the participants administered shocks of up to 300 volts, and about two-thirds applied 450 volts or more. Although they often showed signs of anguish, they felt they had to obey the supervisor. Milgram explained that we are brought up to respect and obey authority figures. But we can choose not to obey when told to

I KNEW IT WAS WRONG...

PEOPLE DO WHAT THEY ARE **TOLD** TO DO.
STANLEY MILGRAM

do **BAD** things?

act against our conscience, or give up our personal responsibility and simply follow orders, which can lead otherwise good people to commit dreadful acts.

Playing a role

While Milgram's experiment showed how people tend to obey authority, Philip Zimbardo looked at how our social circumstances influence our willingness to do bad things. In his famous Stanford prison experiment, he set up a mock prison at Stanford University, and 24 students were randomly assigned the role of either "prisoner" or "guard." The startling thing about the experiment was how quickly and completely the participants adapted to their roles—guards became authoritarian and aggressive, and prisoners became passive. When interviewed later, the guards said they had felt that the role, reinforced by a uniform, club, and handcuffs, gave them power, while the prisoners reported feeling powerless and humiliated. Zimbardo concluded that we all have a tendency to conform to the role that society expects us to play, and social forces have the power to make any one of us capable of doing evil things.

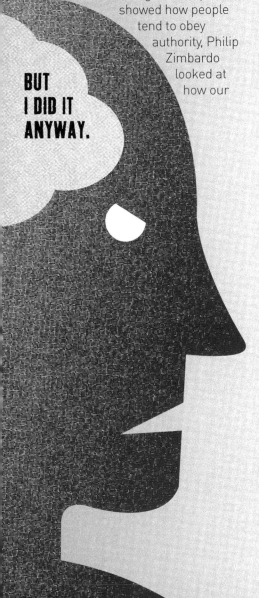

BUT I DID IT ANYWAY.

See also: 28–29, 108–109, 134–135

MANY PEOPLE **OBSERVED** WHAT WAS HAPPENING AND **SAID NOTHING.**

PHiLiP ZiMBARDO

DOCTOR'S ORDERS

An experimenter pretending to be a doctor called 22 nurses, asking them to give a patient 20mg of a drug, which he would sign for later. Although dispensing drugs requires written authorization, and the maximum safe dose was 10mg, 21 of the nurses gave the patient the medicine (which was actually harmless). But in another group of nurses discussing the experiment, all but one said they wouldn't have given the patient the drug.

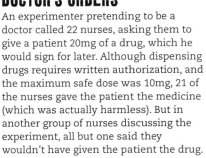

Don't be so

PEOPLE HELP ONE ANOTHER IN VARIOUS WAYS, FROM OFFERING THEIR SEATS TO GIVING MONEY TO CHARITY. BUT EVEN THOUGH THESE ACTS OF KINDNESS APPEAR TO BE FOR THE BENEFIT OF OTHERS, THEY MAY NOT BE COMPLETELY UNSELFISH. PERHAPS TRUE ALTRUISM—HELPING OTHERS WITH NO EXPECTATION OF PERSONAL GAIN—DOESN'T REALLY EXIST.

What's in it for me?

Psychologists disagree about whether or not we are capable of real altruism. Some believe that helping others, especially family members and those in our social group, has the evolutionary function of protecting our own kind. Others argue that all our helping behavior is actually selfish because it allows us to feel good about ourselves and makes us look better to other people; alternatively, it may simply be a way of reducing our own distress at seeing someone else in need. Daniel Batson, however, disagreed that all helping behavior is essentially self-interested, and argued that we have empathetic emotions, such as compassion and tenderness, that lead to a genuine desire to reduce the distress of a victim. And since we all experience this empathy, we are all capable of altruistic behavior.

people are more likely to help others if they are in a good mood—but not if helping is likely to spoil their mood.

The bystander effect

A brutal murder case first stirred up psychologists' interest in helping behavior.

In 1964, 38 people witnessed the stabbing of Kitty Genovese in New York, but none of them offered any help, and only one called the police after the event. The public was shocked that nobody intervened, but psychologists including Philip Zimbardo explained that this was precisely because there were so many witnesses. This phenomenon became known as the "bystander effect"—the more bystanders there are,

FEELING **EMPATHY** FOR A PERSON IN NEED GIVES US THE **MOTIVATION** TO **HELP.**

DANiEL BATSON

the less obligation they feel to get involved. The idea was tested in experiments by John M. Darley and Bibb Latané, who wanted to see if the size of a group influenced the willingness of participants to help someone apparently having an epileptic fit, or to report a smell of smoke in the room. The larger the group, the longer it took for someone to act.

SELFISH!

WOULD YOU HELP SOMEONE IN TROUBLE?

← Lost in the crowd
Studies show that people are less likely to help someone if they are in a large crowd. But Daniel Batson argues that our ability to understand and share the feelings of others—our empathy—should counteract this reluctance.

> ## WHEN **DIFFERENT PEOPLE** WITNESS AN EMERGENCY, ALL ASSUME SOMEONE ELSE WILL HELP.
> **PHILIP ZIMBARDO**

Pros and cons

Darley and Latané argued that bystanders go through a decision-making process when someone is in need of help. Before intervening, they have to respond positively in five stages: They must first notice the event, then interpret it as requiring help, and then assume responsibility. Next, they have to choose a way of helping, and lastly put it into action. A negative response at any stage in the process means the bystander will not help, which explains why most people don't help, rather than why some do. Darley and Latané's theory was later refined to include elements of Batson's ideas about empathy, and ideas about the potential cost and benefit of helping. They described the decision-making process in two stages. The first stage is arousal, an emotional response to the distress and need of the victim. This is followed by a cost-reward stage, when the bystander assesses the pros and cons of intervening. This can often be a dilemma, with the result depending on what type of help is needed as well as the identity of the victim. This model was supported by studies in which experimenters pretended to collapse in a New York subway train. Some carried a cane, and others carried a bottle in a brown paper bag. Help was offered to the "disabled" experimenter 90 percent of the time, but to the "drunk" only 20 percent of the time. Assessing the situation, bystanders may have concluded that the drunk was less deserving of aid, and helping might have been more trouble than it was worth.

See also: 146–147

THE GOOD SAMARITAN

Students were asked to give a talk about the Good Samaritan. When they arrived, some were told that they were late, some that they were just in time, and others that they were early. They were directed to a room, past a man lying in a doorway, clearly in distress. Only 10 percent of those in a rush offered help, compared with 45 percent of those in a moderate hurry, and 63 percent of those with plenty of time. The students in a hurry must have thought that helping wasn't worth the risk of being late.

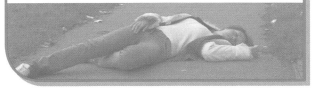

SOLOMON ASCH

1907–1996

Solomon Asch and his family emigrated to New York from Warsaw, Poland, in 1920, when he was 13. After graduating with a science degree, he earned a PhD in psychology under Gestalt psychologist Max Wertheimer. Asch continued his mentor's work in Gestalt psychology, teaching at several American universities, and became one of the pioneers in the field of social psychology. He is most famous for his work on conformity.

PROPAGANDA

After World War II, Asch studied the propaganda used by both sides in their war efforts. Many psychologists believed that the persuasiveness of propaganda depended mainly on the prestige of the person delivering the message. Asch disagreed, saying that people don't blindly accept a message just because of who is saying it, but examine its content and meaning in light of who is telling them.

Asch spoke little English when he arrived in New York, so taught himself by reading Charles Dickens.

CANDID CAMERA

As part of his study into how we tend to conform to other people's behavior, Asch collaborated with the television show *Candid Camera*. Using a hidden camera, an unwitting passenger was filmed getting into a crowded elevator. The people in the elevator were all instructed by Asch to turn the wrong way—to face away from the door— after the stranger entered. Seeing them do this, the stranger also turned toward the back of the elevator.

MAKING AN IMPRESSION

One of Asch's many interests was how people form impressions of others. In one study, he gave participants lists of characteristics of hypothetical people. He found that small differences in the list—for example, describing someone as "warm" rather than "cold"— without changing the other characteristics, led participants to form significantly different overall opinions of people.

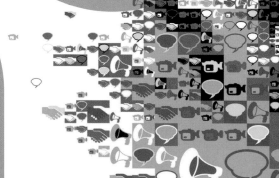

> "The **human mind** is an organ for the **discovery of truths** rather than of **falsehoods**."

METAPHORS

Through his work on impression-forming, Asch became fascinated by the language we use to describe characteristics. He noticed that people use terms such as *cold, warm, sweet,* and *bitter* not only for physical things, but also to describe personality traits. By examining similar figures of speech in languages from all over the world, both ancient and modern, he found that they reflect the way we try to understand people's characteristics.

ATTITUDE

YOUNG PEOPLE ARE IRRESPONSIBLE...

... BUT IF I WANT TO GET THE JOB DONE, I HAVE TO WORK WITH THIS YOUNG MAN.

OUR ATTITUDES, ESPECIALLY THOSE TOWARD OTHER PEOPLE AND IDEAS, ARE OFTEN BASED ON DEEPLY HELD BELIEFS, AND WE'RE RELUCTANT TO CHANGE THEM—SOME MORE THAN OTHERS. ATTITUDES INFLUENCE OUR BEHAVIOR, BUT SOMETIMES WE DO THINGS JUST TO FIT IN, WHEN WHAT WE ACTUALLY THINK HASN'T CHANGED.

What are attitudes?

An attitude is the opinion we have of things, such as other people and their ideas and beliefs—not simply the way we feel about them at any particular time, but in general. Social psychologist Daniel Katz explained that our attitudes toward something are a combination of what we associate with it, its attributes, and how much we consider those to be positive or negative. For example, we may believe that young people are adventurous, and older people cautious, but our attitude toward them depends on whether we think these attributes are good or bad. The beliefs and values that form our attitudes are influenced by our social situation. We tend to imitate and conform to the norms of the culture we're brought up in, and to any groups, such as religious or political organizations, we belong to. Our attitudes have several functions, according to Katz. If they are socially acceptable, they help us gain approval from others. They also help us make consistent judgments

about things, to express what we think, and to defend ourselves against opposing opinions. For example, students who are bad at sports may develop a negative attitude toward all sports, to protect themselves from humiliation.

people are more likely to like other people, objects, and statements if they are introduced to them while eating a meal.

Attitudes and action

Naturally, the way we feel about something affects how we behave. Our attitude toward politics, for example, influences our voting behavior, perhaps our choice of newspaper, and even our selection of friends. It also affects how we interact with people who have different views. But attitudes are not always an accurate indication of how someone will behave. In some situations, people do things that go against their opinions because they feel a need to conform with the views of others, or to obey an authority figure. When people find that their attitude is not acceptable to those around them, there is social pressure for them to act in a certain way, but

problem?

OLD PEOPLE ARE BORING...

... BUT IF I WANT THE JOB, I HAVE TO BE NICE TO THIS OLD GUY.

◉ **Internal conflict**
Sometimes, people act as though they get along and respect each other, but this doesn't mean that they feel like this deep down inside.

this doesn't mean their attitude has changed. Attitudes are not what people do, but what they think and feel.

ATTITUDES ARE A COMBINATION OF BELIEFS AND VALUES.
DANIEL KATZ

Set in our ways?
We find it easier to outwardly conform and hide our opinions than to change the way we think and feel. So do people ever change their attitudes? Since they are formed from beliefs and values that we have built up over a long time, attitudes are deeply held and difficult to change. And some attitudes are more resistant to change than others, especially if we use them defensively to protect ourselves from opposing views. When this is taken to extremes, it leads to prejudice and discrimination against people and ideas, and can give us a feeling of superiority. But, just as attitudes are formed socially based on the norms of our social groups, they can also change when we move into different social circles, or as the attitudes of our group change—as they do over

time. For example, 200 years ago, most people accepted the existence of slavery because this was a socially acceptable attitude at the time. As society changed, so did people's individual attitudes, and today almost nobody would feel they could support the idea of slavery.

BLACK AND WHITE
In the Southern United States in the 1950s, prejudice against black people was the social norm. But in a study of miners, psychologists found that the norm below ground was different. When working in the mine, 80 percent of white miners were friends with black colleagues, but when they got above ground, only 20 percent of them continued to be friendly with the black miners. The white miners were conforming to different norms above and below ground.

The power of PERSUASION

MANY PEOPLE SEEK TO CHANGE OUR OPINIONS. ON A PERSONAL LEVEL, FRIENDS MAY TRY TO CONVINCE US TO DO OR THINK SOMETHING, BUT THERE ARE ALSO ADVERTISERS TRYING TO SELL US PRODUCTS, AND POLITICIANS AND EVANGELISTS HOPING TO INFLUENCE OUR IDEAS. THESE DIFFERENT SOURCES ALL USE SIMILAR TECHNIQUES TO PERSUADE US.

See also: 74–75

Getting the message across

When someone we know tries to make us change our minds, he or she will often present a logical argument for his or her own point of view. But this is not the only thing that will persuade us—we're also influenced by whether or not we like the person, if other people have the same idea, and what we might gain from changing our opinion. The same is true whenever advertisers or public figures try to persuade others. Presenting a good argument is only part of the process.

using someone's name in a conversation will make that person more likely to like you and believe you.

To get the message across, it must have emotional as well as logical appeal, and come from a reliable and trusted source. Those being persuaded must also believe that the message is relevant to them, and be made to feel comfortable with the new idea—it must not conflict with any of their deeply held beliefs.

Tricks of the trade

In the 20th century, advertisers increasingly used the psychology of persuasion to sell products, as advertising techniques began to reflect psychologists' understanding of how attitudes can be changed. After a scandal that lost him his university position, behaviorist psychologist John B. Watson started working at an advertising agency, where he used his knowledge of psychology to sell all kinds of products. Advertisers had known for a long time that simply presenting a good product is not enough, but Watson suggested new ways of persuading consumers. Effective advertising should have an emotional appeal, he believed, and should trigger a response involving love, fear, or rage—for example, it might

FEAR OF THE UNKNOWN

People feel more comfortable with what they know, and tend to feel uneasy about new ideas, especially if they conflict with their own. Social psychologist Robert Zajonc showed people different symbols and found that the more often they saw a particular symbol, the more they came to like it. Repeated exposure makes us more comfortable with things, and our attitude toward them changes.

suggest that a product will make you more attractive to the opposite sex, or that organic produce is safer to eat than processed food. Watson also pioneered the use of product endorsement—using doctors and celebrities to give authority to a message—and market research as a systematic means of finding out how receptive people might be to a new product.

Manipulating minds

Other professionals use the same techniques, not to sell products, but to sell ideas. Political and religious groups, for example, need to persuade people of their ideas and recruit new members. Fear can be a particularly powerful tool to change minds—for instance, in health campaigns to urge people to quit smoking. But fear can also be used to promote extreme views. In a study of Nazi propaganda from the 1930s and 1940s, James A. C. Brown identified the way fear was used to manipulate people's thinking. Playing on the fear of standing out from the crowd,

propaganda limits people's choices, replacing logical argument with a single viewpoint, presented as if it were an unarguable fact, and often scapegoating a stereotypical "enemy" (in this case, Jews). A charismatic leader, such as Adolf Hitler, then repeats the idea as an emotional slogan, effectively "brainwashing" or indoctrinating people. The same techniques have been used by other tyrannical regimes, and also by religious cults. But the power to persuade can be positive, too: In cognitive behavioral therapy, it helps change unhealthy attitudes that can have a damaging effect on a person's mental health.

> ## A FEAR OF BEING A LONE VOICE MAKES PEOPLE WANT TO SUBMERGE THEMSELVES IN THE MASS.
> **JAMES A. C. BROWN**

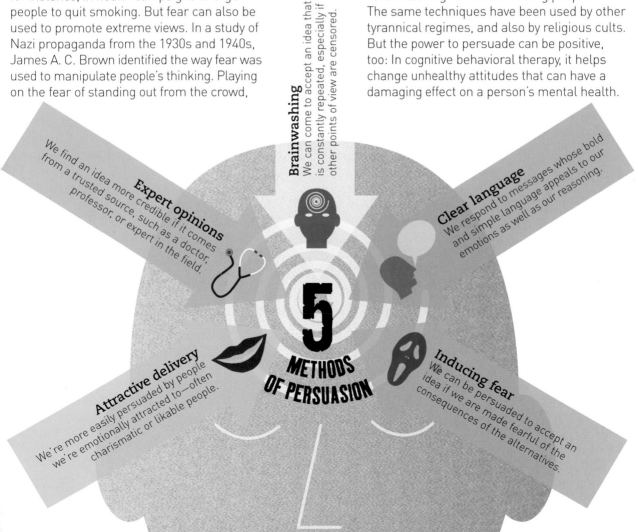

Brainwashing
We can come to accept an idea that is constantly repeated, especially if other points of view are censored.

Expert opinions
We find an idea more credible if it comes from a trusted source, such as a doctor, professor, or expert in the field.

Clear language
We respond to messages whose bold and simple language appeals to our emotions as well as our reasoning.

5 METHODS OF PERSUASION

Attractive delivery
We're more easily persuaded by people we're emotionally attracted to—often charismatic or likable people.

Inducing fear
We can be persuaded to accept an idea if we are made fearful of the consequences of the alternatives.

What makes you

ANGER IS ONE OF OUR BASIC HUMAN EMOTIONS, AND SOMETHING WE ALL FEEL FROM TIME TO TIME. IT CAN COME FROM WITHIN US, THROUGH FRUSTRATION, OR BE TRIGGERED BY SOMETHING IN OUR ENVIRONMENT. LIKE OTHER EMOTIONS, WE ONLY HAVE LIMITED CONTROL OVER ANGER—IT CAN BOIL OVER AND SHOW ITSELF IN AGGRESSION TOWARD OTHERS.

> **AGGRESSION IS ALWAYS A CONSEQUENCE OF FRUSTRATION... AND FRUSTRATION ALWAYS LEADS TO AGGRESSION.**
> JOHN DOLLARD AND NEAL E MiLLER

See also: 26–27, 92–93

Inner anger

More than other animals, humans have learned to control their anger and aggression, but many psychologists believe it is part of human nature. Some take the cynical view that we are basically selfish, and use our aggression to gain power and advantage. Konrad Lorenz explained aggression as an instinct with an evolutionary function, helping us protect our families, resources, and territory from others. Sigmund Freud linked this instinct to an impulse for self-destruction—an inner anger against ourselves, which we repress, but which, when it builds up, can lead to a violent outburst of aggressive behavior toward others. But even though anger and aggression may be an innate part of human nature, Albert Bandura argued that the way we show it—through our aggressive behavior—is something that we learn socially. In his famous Bobo doll experiment, he showed that children imitate the aggressive behavior of adults, leading to concerns that violent movies, television shows, and computer games encourage aggression, especially in young people.

> **research has shown that sports teams who wear black commit more fouls.**

How frustrating

American psychologists John Dollard and Neal E. Miller were also intrigued by the causes of aggressive behavior. They suggested that we become aggressive when we are prevented from achieving something. People feel frustrated that their efforts are being blocked and will direct their aggression toward whatever is getting in their way. Sometimes, if there is nobody responsible for their frustration, or if the problem is due to their own inability, the aggression is directed at an innocent target, called a scapegoat. Dollard and Miller believed that frustration always leads to aggression, but they later refined their

SYMBOLS OF VIOLENCE

In Leonard Berkowitz's study, half of the participants were given electric shocks. They were then given the chance to administer shocks in return. They did this from a room that contained either a gun or a badminton racquet. Those who had received shocks unsurprisingly gave more back, but the most shocks were given by those who had received shocks and were also exposed to the gun.

ANGRY?

theory to show that there are degrees of frustration: It is more likely to produce aggression when it comes out of the blue, and when it seems that the person responsible for the frustration is being obstructive for no good reason.

Dangerous triggers

Leonard Berkowitz, however, felt that frustration did not fully explain aggressive behavior. In his opinion, frustration causes anger rather than aggression, and anger is just one form of psychological pain that leads to aggressive behavior. Any form of pain—physical as well as psychological—can provoke our aggression, but there has to be another external factor, a cue, to make us react with aggressive behavior (see Symbols of Violence,

> **THE FINGER PULLS THE TRIGGER, BUT THE TRIGGER MAY ALSO BE PULLING THE FINGER.**
>
> **LEONARD BERKOWITZ**

left). Berkowitz argued that we associate aggressive behavior with certain things, such as weapons. When we experience these cues in our environment, it brings aggressive thoughts and feelings into our minds, which may trigger violent or aggressive behavior in response to our discomfort.

Ready to erupt ❯

We get angry when we're frustrated, but also when we're exposed to certain cues. These may include obvious things such as weapons, as well as loud noises, bad smells, or uncomfortable temperatures.

SAW A GUN

ANNOYING NOISE

REALLY BAD SMELL

LOST THE GAME

TRAFFIC JAM

WE EXPLODE FOR ALL KINDS OF REASONS...

STANLEY MILGRAM

1933–1984

The son of a Jewish Hungarian baker and his Romanian wife, Stanley Milgram was born in New York City. He was an excellent student, and went on to study political science before earning a PhD in social psychology at Harvard. Milgram became famous for his experiments on obedience while teaching at Yale in the 1960s. He was working as a professor in New York when he died of a heart attack in 1984.

CREATING CONTROVERSY

In Milgram's most famous experiment, participants were ordered to give electric shocks to a learner who answered questions wrong. Many participants obeyed instructions to give increasingly severe shocks, suggesting that most people will do anything if they are told to do so. The shocks were actually fake, but the fact that participants believed they were hurting someone made the experiment very controversial.

THE LOST LETTER

In an experiment exploring people's attitudes, Milgram and his colleagues left stamped but unmailed letters in public places. The letters were addressed to various organizations, some to obviously "good" institutions, such as Medical Research Associates, and others to "bad" groups, such as the Friends of the Nazi Party. People's attitudes toward these organizations were revealed by whether or not they mailed the letters.

THE LOST CHILD

An apparently lost child was sent out by Milgram into the streets of America in an experiment to see how many people would offer help. The child told passersby, "I'm lost. Can you call my house?" Milgram found that the reaction varied from place to place. In small towns, people were generally sympathetic, and 72 percent offered help. But in the big city many ignored the plea, and less than half tried to help, often swerving to avoid the child.

In high school, one of Milgram's classmates was Philip Zimbardo, who also became a controversial social psychologist.

"The **disappearance** of a sense of responsibility is the most far-reaching consequence of submission to **authority**."

A BAD INFLUENCE?

In a study of the influence of television on antisocial behavior, Milgram showed people an episode of the hospital drama *Medical Center*, with some groups seeing a different ending from others. In one version, a central character steals money; in another, he gives it to charity. Milgram then put the participants in similar situations and observed whether they imitated the actions of the character. He found that most people, even those who had watched the scene of theft, did not steal any money themselves.

Are you in the

HUMANS ARE SOCIAL ANIMALS, AND ORGANIZE THEMSELVES INTO GROUPS TO DO THINGS THEY CAN'T DO ALONE. SOME GROUPS ARE FORMED WHEN LIKE-MINDED PEOPLE GET TOGETHER, WHILE OTHERS CONSIST OF PEOPLE WITH DIFFERENT OPINIONS. EITHER WAY, TO WORK EFFICIENTLY GROUP MEMBERS HAVE TO AGREE ON A COURSE OF ACTION AND ACT AS ONE.

> IT IS NOT THE SIMILARITY OR DISSIMILARITY OF INDIVIDUALS THAT CONSTITUTES A GROUP, BUT INTERDEPENDENCE OF FATE.
>
> KURT LEWIN

Working together

One of the first psychologists to study how people come together in groups was Kurt Lewin, who coined the term "group dynamics" to describe how groups and their individual members behave and develop. His ideas were influenced by the Gestalt psychology notion that "the whole is different from the sum of its parts," which suggests that groups of people can achieve things that individuals cannot. But individual members of a group may each have different opinions, and to work together as a team they have to agree on common goals, or come to a consensus. Consensus within a group is considered important, even in Western societies where individuality is regarded highly, and we rely on group institutions such as juries and committees to make fair and correct decisions.

> we come up with more creative ideas alone, rather than in groups.

Thinking together

Our natural desire to conform can help a group reach agreements and build team spirit, but it has a negative side, too. Social psychologist Irving Janis

pointed out that this need for conformity can lead to a loss of individuality. Group members may feel that they should go along with what the others think, and there can be an element of obedience as well as conformity, when individuals feel pressure to accept the decisions of the group. There is then a danger of what sociologist William H. Whyte called "groupthink"—when the pressure to conform overrides independent critical thinking. Individual members of a group not only go along with the decisions of the group; they also come to believe that these decisions are always right, and sometimes bad decisions are unanimously endorsed. Another risk is that members begin to feel that their group can do no wrong and is better than other groups, causing conflict between "in-groups" and "out-groups."

Allowing dissent

Janis recognized the problems of groupthink, but felt that it could be avoided. It is most likely to develop when team spirit becomes more important than the opinions

> GROUPTHINK HOLDS THAT GROUP VALUES ARE NOT ONLY EXPEDIENT BUT RIGHT AND GOOD AS WELL.
>
> WILLIAM H. WHYTE

IN CROWD?

INDEPENDENT THOUGHT CAN BE SWALLOWED UP BY GROUP MENTALITY.

⊘ **Big fish, little fish?**
Similar or like-minded individuals are more likely to form groups. Once in the group, members risk losing their individuality and blindly following the majority, sometimes with sinister consequences.

See also: 76–77, 138–139

of individual members. It's also likely to form if the group is made up of like-minded people to begin with, and if they are faced with a difficult decision. To prevent groupthink, Janis proposed a system of organization that encourages independent thinking. The leader of the group should appear to be impartial, so that members do not feel any pressure to obey. Furthermore, he or she should get the group to examine all the options, and to consult people outside the group, too. Disagreement, Janis argued, is actually a good thing, and he suggested that members should be asked to play "devil's advocate"—introducing an alternative point of view in order to provoke discussion. In addition to ensuring that the group comes to more rational and fair decisions, allowing

members to retain their individuality creates a healthier team spirit than the state of groupthink, which results from conformity and obedience.

IN MY GANG

In an experiment in the 1950s, Muzafer Sherif divided a group of boys at summer camp into two teams. Unaware of the other team, the boys bonded among their own. Later, the teams were introduced and had to compete in a series of contests. All the boys felt that their team was better than the other, and signs of conflict emerged between the teams. Most of the boys also said their best friends were members of their own team, even though many of them had best friends in the other team before the experiment.

PEOPLE HAVE TO WORK TOGETHER IN GROUPS IN ALL KINDS OF SITUATIONS—IN BUSINESS, POLITICS, AND LEISURE ACTIVITIES SUCH AS SPORTS AND MUSIC. THE INDIVIDUAL MEMBERS NEED TO WORK AS A TEAM TO FUNCTION EFFECTIVELY, AND THIS HAPPENS BEST IF THE GROUP IS ORGANIZED. IN MOST ORGANIZATIONS, THERE IS ALSO A NEED FOR SOME FORM OF LEADERSHIP.

Team spirit

When a group of people are working on a task, it's important that the individual members work as a team and collaborate to achieve common goals. Kurt Lewin, who pioneered research into how groups behave, showed that, to function as a team, each person must feel like a necessary part of the group. If all individuals realize that their well-being is dependent on the well-being of the group as a whole, they are more likely to take a fair share of responsibility for the team's welfare. In order for everyone to make a contribution, members need to be organized according to their strengths and weaknesses. Australian psychologist Elton Mayo found that

needs that leaders should consider. The first, task needs, are the things that have to be achieved to get the job done. There are also group needs, such as making sure people collaborate effectively and resolving any disputes that arise. Finally, individual needs are what each member of the team wants

SOME MANAGERS DON'T HAVE MUCH FAITH IN THEIR TEAM—THEY ASSUME THAT TEAM MEMBERS ARE LAZY AND HAVE TO BE TOLD EXACTLY WHAT TO DO.

X

What makes a

industrial workers informally sorted themselves into groups, and one person emerged as a leader who organized the group and built "team spirit." Other hierarchies may be more formal, but all are structured so that each member has a place in the group under a leadership that inspires teamwork.

WHEN **AUTHORITY** DOESN'T WORK, DON'T USE **LESS OR MORE.** USE ANOTHER MEANS OF **INFLUENCE.**
DOUGLAS MCGREGOR

Follow the leader

Mayo also discovered that working together is a human social need, and belonging to a group is more important than any reward for doing a task. For leadership to be effective, it has to recognize the social needs of team members as well as making sure they do their job. Psychologists since Mayo have identified three different kinds of

About two-thirds of workers say the most stressful thing about their job is their boss.

to get out of the job. Balancing the different needs helps build a team in which members feel involved and committed, and take pride in the organization.

Management styles

A leader can encourage the members of his or her team to work together on a task in many different ways. Some leaders take an authoritarian approach, telling subordinates what they should and shouldn't

THERE ARE TWO STYLES OF LEADERSHIP...

OTHER MANAGERS TRUST THAT THEIR TEAM MEMBERS ARE MOTIVATED AND CAPABLE, AND LET THEM GET ON WITH THE JOB WITH LITTLE INTERFERENCE.

Y

See also: 136–137

WINNING team?

do. Others are more democratic and consult the team, and some simply let members get on with what they're doing. The leader's attitude toward his or her team also determines management style, according to American management expert Douglas McGregor. He suggested that there are two theories of leadership in business: theory X and theory Y. In theory X, a manager assumes workers are lazy, unambitious, and unwilling to take on responsibility, so he or she adopts a strict, authoritarian leadership style. In theory Y, however, a manager assumes workers are motivated, ambitious, and self-disciplined, and thus adopts a more collaborative style. While McGregor's ideas primarily relate to business

management, and especially human resource management, the same two types of leadership styles can be seen in teams of all kinds.

THE HAWTHORNE EFFECT

In the 1930s, Elton Mayo studied workers in the Hawthorne Electric Plant in Chicago. He found that productivity increased when he raised the lighting levels in the factory. When he lowered the lighting again, rather than returning to the original level, productivity increased further, and raising the lighting once more increased it yet again. Workers responded not to the lighting, but to the fact that someone was interested in what they were doing.

MANY OF OUR LEISURE PURSUITS INVOLVE COMPETITIVE SPORTS AND GAMES, WHETHER WE ARE PARTICIPANTS OR SPECTATORS. THE PRESSURES OF COMPETITION AND BEING IN FRONT OF AN AUDIENCE MAY OR MAY NOT HELP ATHLETES DO THEIR BEST. BEING A MEMBER OF A TEAM CAN ALSO INFLUENCE HOW WELL AN INDIVIDUAL PERFORMS.

Can you PERFORM under

competitive instinct that spurs us to perform better. Later studies have shown that rivalry actually has a physical effect too, and is associated with physical changes such as increased heart rate and testosterone levels, which enhance our performance.

Competitive streak

One of the first psychologists to examine the psychology of sports was Norman Triplett, who at the end of the 19th century conducted experiments to see how competition affects our performance. He noticed that cyclists rode faster when competing against others than when they were riding alone against the clock. To test whether or not competition actually improves performance, he devised an experiment in which children pulled a flag on a rope by turning a reel, either alone or competing in pairs. He found that they consistently recorded faster times when competing, and concluded that we have a

> The joy we feel when our team wins lasts longer than our despair when we lose.

Spectator sport

Other psychologists studying performance in sports noticed that participants did better not only when competing against somebody else, but also when they were simply doing something at the same time as other people, and even when they were just being watched by others. Gordon Allport called these the "coaction effect" and "audience effect," and explained that we do things better in the presence of others, but not necessarily in competition. However, Robert Zajonc and others found that this was not always the case. When we do something we are already good at— a simple task or a skill we have practiced such as kicking a ball into a goal—we do it better with others there. But if it is something difficult, such as a tricky shot, the presence of other people has

ROACH RACING

It's not just humans who are affected by having an audience. Experiments with cockroaches in 1969 showed that they found it more difficult to find their way around a maze when there were other cockroaches present than when they were alone. In the easier task of a straight run, however, they ran faster in the presence of other cockroaches than on their own.

PRESSURE?

LEARNING IS **IMPAIRED** BUT PERFORMANCE IS **FACILITATED** BY THE PRESENCE OF **SPECTATORS.**

ROBERT ZAJONC

the opposite effect. We need to concentrate more on tasks that challenge us, and we are more likely to perform badly if we are distracted by people watching.

Letting others do the work

The presence of others is, of course, a crucial factor in team sports and activities. We have to not only perform well as individuals, but cooperate as a team. And although the presence of others and the element of competition may improve our performance, there is also a downside to working in a group. Individuals in a team tend to perform worse as the size of the group increases—especially if it's difficult to see how much effort each person is putting in. For example, in a tug-of-war, the more people there are on a team, the less effort each person will make to achieve an overall result. Bibb Latané described this effect of relying on others to put effort in as "social loafing."

WE HURDLE BETTER IF PEOPLE ARE WATCHING...

BUT ONLY   IF WE HAVE PRACTICED   HURDLING...

AND WE HAVE TO BE CAREFUL NOT TO GET   *DISTRACTED!*

Under pressure

We often perform better when others are watching us, but only if we're doing something we're good at. If not, an audience can be off-putting, and may even hurt our performance.

COMPETITION USUALLY IMPROVES AN INDIVIDUAL'S PERFORMANCE.

See also: 26–27, 84–85, 104–105

ARE YOU THINKING

THERE ARE OBVIOUS PHYSICAL DIFFERENCES BETWEEN GUYS AND GIRLS, BUT IT'S LESS CLEAR WHETHER OR NOT THERE ARE ALSO PSYCHOLOGICAL DIFFERENCES BETWEEN THE SEXES. IF THERE ARE, DO THEY COME FROM HOW GUYS AND GIRLS ARE TREATED, OR DO THEIR BRAINS WORK IN DIFFERENT WAYS?

Do GUYS think

Gender conformity

The rise of feminism in the 1950s and 1960s prompted an interest in the psychological differences between the sexes. French philosopher Simone de Beauvoir argued that although we may be born either male or female, society's ideas of what is masculine or feminine are forced upon us—and, since most societies are male-dominated, femininity is usually seen as submissive and emotional. Many feminists agreed, and made a distinction between sex (what makes us physically a man or woman) and gender

the parts of the brain that control aggression are larger in women than in men.

(the differences in thought and behavior dictated by society). Developmental psychologist Albert Bandura confirmed this idea, suggesting that guys and girls behave differently because they're treated differently—they learn the gender stereotypes socially, from people around them. And society's attitudes prevail as they grow up, so that we view people negatively if they behave differently from the gender stereotypes. Psychologist Alice Eagly showed that competent women in particular are seen in a negative light if they show their abilities in a traditionally masculine way—Margaret Thatcher, for example, became known as "the Iron Lady" for her strong leadership as British prime minister in the 1980s.

On an intellectual level

But is there any underlying reason for these gender stereotypes? Are there any real psychological gender differences?

EVERY KNOWN HUMAN SOCIETY HAS RULES ABOUT GENDER.

ELEANOR E. MACCOBY

Eleanor E. Maccoby thought there weren't, and showed that nearly all of the traditional ideas about gender are, in fact, myths. For example, she found no evidence that guys have different intellectual abilities than girls. But there was one difference that was difficult to explain: Girls consistently did better at

like GIRLS?

school than guys. This clashed with the traditional stereotype of the male drive for achievement and supposed aptitude for intellectual tasks. Maccoby argued that the real difference was not in ability, but that girls, especially teenage girls, are more disciplined than guys, and put more effort into academic studies.

Male and female brains?

Some psychologists, however, believe that there are real differences in the way the sexes think and behave that are not socially learned. Evolutionary psychologists argue that innate differences lead women naturally to care for their families, and men to protect and provide for them. And recently Simon Baron-Cohen proposed a theory that there are "male brains" and "female brains" (although these do not necessarily correspond to a person's physical sex). He suggested that female brains are more empathizing, able to recognize and respond to other people's thoughts and feelings, while male brains are systemizing, able to analyze and deal with mechanical and abstract systems and rules. Women tend to score more highly on the scale of empathizing, while men tend to score more highly on the scale of systemizing. Although Baron-Cohen's research appears to provide some grounds for gender stereotyping, there is by no means a clear-cut division between the two sexes: Many men have empathizing brains, and many women have systemizing brains. A significant number of people think that they have characteristics associated with the opposite sex, and some even feel that they have been born with the wrong body. Our ideas of the differences between men and women have traditionally been black and white, but it seems that it's actually a very gray area.

BABY X EXPERIMENT

In several studies in the 1970s, adults were shown a young baby, Baby X. Some were told it was a boy, some were told it was a girl, and others were not told its sex. Their reactions—how they played with the baby, and interpreted its responses to toys such as dolls or cars—showed that their attitudes were influenced by which sex they believed it was.

Why do people fall in **LOVE?**

Both men and women are naturally more attracted to people with symmetrical faces.

See also: 14–15, 94–95

AMONG OUR BASIC HUMAN NEEDS IS THE NEED FOR OTHER PEOPLE. WE NEED THE COMPANIONSHIP OF FRIENDS, BUT ALSO THE AFFECTION AND INTIMACY OF A CLOSER RELATIONSHIP. PSYCHOLOGISTS HAVE TRIED TO DISCOVER HOW WE CHOOSE OUR PARTNERS, WHY WE ARE ATTRACTED TO THEM, AND WHAT LOVE IS.

Different kinds of love

Our relationships with other people help make our lives meaningful, and friendships play an important part in this. But we also form more committed relationships that are different from friendship—although we may have several friends at once, we normally have only one romantic partner. This kind of exclusive, one-on-one relationship is usually associated with love rather than friendship. Some psychologists believe that this kind of love has an evolutionary purpose, helping us choose a mate to have children with, and keeping couples together in order to bring up offspring. Others, including John Bowlby, have described love as a form of attachment, similar to the attachment of a child to its parent, with elements of caregiving as well as sexual attraction. But there are different kinds of love, from passionate, romantic love to contented companionship. And there are various kinds of committed relationships, too: In Western societies, individuals can choose their own partners, but in many cultures marriages are arranged by their parents. In other societies, polygamy (a marriage that includes more than two partners) is considered normal, and a significant proportion of relationships worldwide are same-sex.

Love and attraction

Robert Sternberg examined the different kinds of love and identified three basic factors involved in a loving relationship: intimacy, passion, and commitment. Romantic love, he said, involves intimacy and passion, but little commitment, whereas companionate love has less passion, and involves a combination of

GROWING OLD TOGETHER

Participants in a study by Robert Zajonc were shown photographs of people in the first year of marriage, and the same couples 25 years later. They noticed that the couples became more facially similar as they got older together. This may be because people tend to choose partners physically similar to themselves, or because they imitate one another's facial expressions.

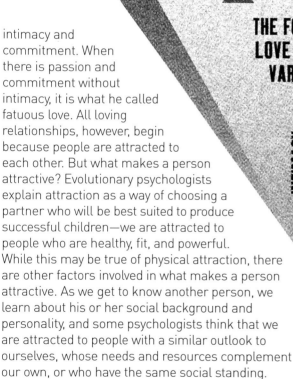

PASSION

COMMITMENT

INTIMACY

THE FORMULA OF LOVE HAS MANY VARIATIONS.

Love triangle
Robert Sternberg thought that loving relationships involve three factors, and the different combinations of these factors determine the type of love in a relationship. The strongest relationships are built on all three elements.

intimacy and commitment. When there is passion and commitment without intimacy, it is what he called fatuous love. All loving relationships, however, begin because people are attracted to each other. But what makes a person attractive? Evolutionary psychologists explain attraction as a way of choosing a partner who will be best suited to produce successful children—we are attracted to people who are healthy, fit, and powerful. While this may be true of physical attraction, there are other factors involved in what makes a person attractive. As we get to know another person, we learn about his or her social background and personality, and some psychologists think that we are attracted to people with a similar outlook to ourselves, whose needs and resources complement our own, or who have the same social standing.

Staying together
Unfortunately, not all intimate relationships last beyond the initial period of attraction. This is just the first of several stages in a relationship, and can be followed by falling in love, making a commitment to each other, and finally settling into a stable life together. For a relationship to become a lasting one, Sternberg argued that it must rely on more than one of the elements of intimacy, passion, and commitment, and should ideally be a combination of all three. But even long-term, loving relationships can break down, for a variety of reasons. Some are unstable because of differences in age or socioeconomic background, but often couples simply grow apart. And even in the most loving relationships there will be conflict, and how it's resolved may determine whether or not the partnership will survive.

ATTACHMENT CHARACTERIZES HUMAN RELATIONSHIPS FROM CRADLE TO GRAVE.

JOHN BOWLBY

THE AMOUNT OF LOVE ONE EXPERIENCES DEPENDS ON THE ABSOLUTE STRENGTH OF INTIMACY, PASSION, AND COMMITMENT.

ROBERT STERNBERG

People can often be very cruel to one another on the Internet. It seems that anonymity has a role to play, allowing people to behave as if there are no consequences to their actions. Psychologists have argued that social networking sites need to expose these offenders to show that online bullying is unacceptable.

ONLINE BULLYING

TO THE RESCUE

Strangely, the more people who see someone in distress, the less likely they are to help. This is called the "bystander effect" because each person assumes that someone else will provide assistance. If you are ever in trouble, point to a single person and say, "help me."

Social psychology in the
REAL WORLD

Psychologists have observed that simply being close to people is enough to make you like them. Students who live on the same floor are far more likely to be friends with one another than those from different floors, even if they have been assigned their rooms at random.

FAMILIAR FRIENDS

ONE OF US

We are more easily influenced by people we like—this is why salespeople flatter their customers. We also tend to trust and believe people who seem similar to ourselves. Politicians often mimic the language of their audiences and dress in a casual way in order to appeal to voters.

Some psychologists believe that we conform for evolutionary reasons. Fitting in with the crowd by wearing fashionable clothes or liking popular bands is more likely to lead to social acceptance. Without this, we might struggle to find partners to mate with. So, on a certain level, conforming makes us more attractive.

FINDING A MATE

STAGE FRIGHT

Even top bands have to put in hours of practice before performing live. Having an audience may affect the way we perform. If a task is simple, or you are an expert, you will perform better. If it is challenging, and you are not an expert, you are likely to perform worse.

Social psychologists study the way people interact with one another, form groups, and exert pressure on others. Their findings help to explain our relationships with friends and loved ones, and can be used by individuals and organizations, such as politicians and advertisers, to influence our behavior.

If you want people to like you, make sure your handshake is warm. Researchers discovered that they could influence people's impressions of others by changing the temperature of their hands. Warm hands result in impressions of personal warmth.

WARM TOUCH

ADVERTISING TRICKS

Have you noticed how television commercials for boring things tend to be wacky? Advertisers have realized that it can be better to persuade people using humor rather than reason. The duller the product, the less people listen to rational arguments.

Directory of psychologists

Mary Ainsworth (1913–1999) See 30–31

Gordon Allport (1897–1867) See 88–89

Elliot Aronson (1932–)
Elliott Aronson grew up in poverty in Massachusetts, during the Great Depression. He began studying economics at college, but changed to psychology after accidentally wandering into one of Abraham Maslow's lectures. He is noted for his research on prejudice and extreme behavior, and is the only person to have won all three awards offered by the American Psychological Association—for writing, teaching, and research.

Albert Bandura (1925–)
Best known for his Bobo doll experiment and social learning theory, Albert Bandura was born to Polish parents in a small town in Alberta, Canada. After earning his doctorate at the University of Iowa, Bandura taught at Stanford University. He was the president of the American Psychological Association for 1974.

Aaron Beck (1921–)
Aaron Beck was born in Rhode Island, the son of Russian immigrants. After suffering a serious illness at the age of eight, he decided to train as a doctor. Beck attended Brown University and Yale medical school, before qualifying as a psychiatrist and working at the University of Pennsylvania. In 1994, he founded the Beck Institute for Cognitive Behavior Therapy with his daughter, Judith Beck. He is widely regarded as the father of cognitive therapy, and his pioneering methods are used to treat depression.

Colin Blakemore (1944–)
Colin Blakemore is a professor of neuroscience at the University of Oxford and the University of London, and was formerly the chief executive of the British Medical Research Council. His research focuses on vision and brain development, and he is well known for his work on the concept of neuroplasticity, as well as his vocal support for the use of animal testing in medical research.

Gordon H. Bower (1932–)
Gordon H. Bower is best known for his contributions to cognitive psychology, particularly his work on human memory. He was brought up in Ohio, and was introduced to the works of Sigmund Freud in high school. He went on to earn a degree in psychology from Case Western Reserve University in Cleveland, switching to Yale for his PhD. He taught at Stanford University, and was awarded the National Medal of Science in 2005.

John Bowlby (1907–1990)
Born in London, England, into an upper-middle-class family, John Bowlby was raised mostly by nannies and was sent to boarding school at the age of seven—experiences that were to influence his later work. He studied psychology at Trinity College, Cambridge, and later qualified as a psychoanalyst. He worked for many years as the director of the Tavistock Clinic in London, and is noted for his pioneering work on attachment theory.

Donald Broadbent (1926–1993) See 70–71

Jerome Bruner (1915–)
A pioneer of the cognitive psychology movement, Jerome Bruner was born in New York City to Polish parents. He studied at Duke University in North Carolina, and earned his doctorate at Harvard. During World War II, he served in the US Army. In 1960, he founded the Center for Cognitive Studies with George Armitage Miller, and he was the president of the American Psychological Association for 1965.

Noam Chomsky (1928–)
Widely known as one of the fathers of modern linguistics, Noam Chomsky is also a philosopher and social activist, and has authored more than 100 books. He earned his bachelor's, master's, and doctoral degrees at the University of Pennsylvania, and later taught at the Massachusetts Institute of Technology. He has received numerous awards for his work, and has been granted honorary degrees from universities around the world.

Mihály Csíkszentmihályi (1934–)
Hungarian psychologist Mihály Csíkszentmihályi was born in Fiume, Italy (now Rijeka, Croatia). He was inspired to study psychology as a teenager after attending a talk by Carl Jung. He moved to the United States to study at the University of Chicago, where he later became head of the psychology department. Now at the University of California, Csíkszentmihályi is best known for his research into happiness and particularly for his theory of "flow."

Hermann Ebbinghaus (1850–1909)
Ebbinghaus was born in Barmen, Germany, into a family of wealthy merchants. He studied at the University of Bonn and became a professor at Berlin University, where he established two psychology laboratories. He is best known for being the first psychologist to study learning and memory systematically, which he achieved by carrying out experiments on himself. He taught until his death from pneumonia at the age of 59.

Paul Ekman (1934–)
American psychologist Paul Ekman began studying at the University of Chicago at the age of 15, where he became interested in Sigmund Freud and psychotherapy. He earned a PhD in clinical psychology at Adelphi University on Long Island, and spent years researching nonverbal communication at the University of California. He has received numerous awards and was a pioneer in the study of emotions and their relation to facial expressions.

Albert Ellis (1913–2007)

Albert Ellis was born into a Jewish family in Pennsylvania. He had a difficult childhood because his mother suffered from bipolar disorder. He worked as an author before studying clinical psychology at Columbia University. There, he was influenced by Sigmund Freud, but later broke away from psychoanalysis and led the shift toward cognitive behavioral therapy. He continued to publish articles and books up until his death at the age of 93.

Erik Erikson (1902–1994)

Erik Erikson coined the term "identity crisis" after struggling with his own identity issues. Born in Frankfurt, Germany, he never knew his biological father, and was brought up by his mother and stepfather. He worked as an art teacher, then trained under Anna Freud as a psychoanalyst. He won a Pulitzer Prize and a National Book Award for his writings, and although he lacked even a bachelor's degree, he served as a professor at Harvard, Yale, and the University of California, Berkeley.

Hans Eysenck (1916–1997)

Hans Eysenck was born in Berlin, Germany. His parents separated soon after his birth and he was raised by his maternal grandmother. He moved to England to study and received his PhD from University College, London, where he later founded and headed the Institute of Psychiatry. Eysenck was a strong critic of psychoanalysis as a form of therapy, preferring behavior therapy, and he is best known for his work on intelligence and personality.

Leon Festinger (1919–1989)

Leon Festinger was born in New York to Russian immigrant parents. He graduated from the City College of New York, then studied for his doctorate under Kurt Lewin at the University of Iowa. He is noted for his cognitive dissonance theory, which he proposed after infiltrating a cult. He is also credited with advancing the use of laboratory experiments in social psychology.

Sigmund Freud (1856–1939) See 102–103

Nico Frijda (1927–)

Nico Frijda was born in Amsterdam into a Jewish family. He lived in hiding during his childhood to avoid the Nazi persecution of the Jews during World War II. Frijda was awarded a PhD from Gemeente Universiteit, Amsterdam, for his thesis on facial expressions. He has devoted his career to human emotions, and said that he was inspired to study the topic as a student, after being in love with "a very expressive girl."

J. J. Gibson (1904–1979)

James Jerome Gibson was born in Ohio. He received his PhD from Princeton University and taught for many years at Smith College in Massachusetts. From 1942 to 1945, Gibson served in World War II, directing the US Air Force Research Unit in Aviation Psychology. He returned to Smith College to research visual perception, and is considered one of the most important 20th-century psychologists in this field.

Donald Hebb (1904–1985)

Donald Hebb was born in Nova Scotia, Canada. While working as a teacher, he encountered the works of Sigmund Freud, William James, and John B. Watson, which led him to become a part-time psychology student at McGill University. He earned his doctorate under Karl Lashley at both the University of Chicago and Harvard. Hebb was a pioneer in biological psychology, noted for his work on how the function of neurons relates to learning. He was the president of the American Psychological Association for 1960.

William James (1842–1910)

Born into a wealthy and influential New York family, William James initially pursued a career as a painter before developing an interest in science. After qualifying as a doctor at Harvard, he taught there for nearly his entire career, and established the first psychology courses in the United States, as well as founding a psychology laboratory. He is remembered for the central role he played in establishing psychology as a truly scientific discipline.

Carl Jung (1875–1961)

Carl Jung was born in a small Swiss village and studied medicine at the University of Basel. He famously collaborated with Sigmund Freud for years, but the pair eventually grew apart over theoretical differences. Jung traveled widely across Africa, America, and India, studying native people. He proposed and developed the concepts of the extroverted and introverted personality types and the collective unconscious.

Daniel Kahneman (1934–)

Daniel Kahneman was born into a Lithuanian Jewish family and was brought up in France. While working toward a science degree, he was introduced to the work of Kurt Lewin, which led him to earn a PhD in psychology at the University of California. Noted for his work on the psychology of human judgment and decision-making, he has received a number of awards, including the Presidential Medal of Freedom in 2013.

Daniel Katz (1903–1998)

Daniel Katz was a social psychologist best known for his studies on racial stereotyping, prejudice, and attitude change. Born in New Jersey, he earned his master's degree from the University at Buffalo and his PhD from Syracuse University. He was a professor of psychology at the University of Michigan and received numerous awards, including the Lewin Award and the Gold Medal of the American Psychological Association.

Lawrence Kohlberg (1927–1987)

Lawrence Kohlberg was born in Bronxville, New York. He worked as a sailor after leaving high school, before enrolling at the University of Chicago and earning a bachelor's degree in just one year. He expanded upon Jean Piaget's work to form a theory that explained the development of moral reasoning, and he taught at both Yale and Harvard Universities after receiving his doctorate.

Wolfgang Köhler (1887–1967)

Wolfgang Köhler was a key figure in the development of Gestalt psychology. He studied at various colleges in Germany before completing a PhD in Berlin. He served as director of the Psychological Institute there until 1935, when, as an outspoken critic of Hitler's Nazi government, he emigrated to the United States. He taught at several American universities and was the president of the American Psychological Association for 1959.

Kurt Lewin (1890–1947)

Kurt Lewin was born into a middle-class Jewish family in Prussia (present-day Poland) and grew up in Berlin, Germany. He studied medicine and biology before serving in the German army during World War I. After suffering injuries, he returned to Berlin to complete his PhD and was influenced by Gestalt psychology. Known as the father of modern social psychology, especially for his work on group dynamics, he taught at several American universities before dying at the age of 57 of a heart attack.

Elizabeth Loftus (1944–) See 62–63

Eleanor E. Maccoby (1917–)

Best known for her work on the psychology of sex differences, developmental psychologist Eleanor Emmons Maccoby is from Tacoma, Washington, and earned her PhD from the University of Michigan. She taught at Harvard before moving to Stanford University, where she became the first woman to serve as chair of the psychology department. The American Psychological Association annually delivers an award in her name.

Abraham Maslow (1908–1970)

Abraham Maslow was born to Jewish parents who emigrated from Russia to the United States. His parents forced him to study law, but Maslow later switched to psychology and earned his PhD at the University of Wisconsin, where the behaviorist Harry Harlow served as his doctoral adviser. Maslow's work focused on human needs and the ability to reach one's full potential. He was elected president of the American Psychological Association for 1968.

Rollo May (1909–1994)

Born in Ohio, Rollo May had a difficult childhood after his parents divorced and his sister was diagnosed with schizophrenia. He earned a degree in English and worked as a teacher in Greece before serving briefly as a church minister back in the United States. He left the ministry to pursue a career in psychology, and went on to receive the first PhD in clinical psychology ever awarded by Columbia University. He is noted for his work on anxiety and depression.

Stanley Milgram (1933–1984) See 134–135

George Armitage Miller (1920–2012)

George Armitage Miller was one of the founders of cognitive psychology, known for his work on human memory. Born in South Carolina, he first studied speech pathology and then earned a PhD in psychology at Harvard. He worked at Harvard, the Massachusetts Institute of Technology, and Rockefeller University before settling at Princeton. In 1969, he was the president of the American Psychological Society, and in 1991 he received the National Medal of Science.

Fritz Perls (1893–1970)

Frederick "Fritz" Perls was born in Berlin, Germany. After serving in the German army during World War I, he studied medicine and then psychiatry. He emigrated to South Africa where, with his wife, psychologist Laura Posner, he started a psychoanalytic training institute. After moving to the United States, they established the New York Institute for Gestalt Therapy, before moving again to California.

Jean Piaget (1896–1980)

Born in Switzerland, Jean Piaget was always interested in the natural world and published his first scientific paper at the age of 11. After earning a PhD in zoology, he began lecturing and publishing papers in psychology and philosophy. Recognized for his research on children's cognitive development, he received the Erasmus Prize in 1972, the Balzan Prize in 1978, and honorary degrees from all over the world.

Laura Posner (1905–1990) See Fritz Perls, above

Vilayanur Ramachandran (1951–) See 44–45

Santiago Ramón y Cajal (1852–1934) See 48–49

Carl Rogers (1902–1987)

Born into a strict Protestant family in Illinois, Carl Rogers's theories were based on his belief that people can realize their full potential and achieve mental well-being. He worked at the Universities of Ohio, Chicago, and Wisconsin, and was the president of the American Psychological Association for 1947. Rogers's last years were devoted to applying his theories in places of social conflict, such as Northern Ireland and South Africa, and he was nominated for the Nobel Peace Prize in 1987.

Dorothy Rowe (1930–)

Dorothy Rowe is a clinical psychologist and writer whose area of interest is depression. She was born in New South Wales, Australia, and studied psychology at Sydney University. She later emigrated to Britain, completed her PhD, and established and headed the Lincolnshire Department of Clinical Psychology. Now based in London, she has contributed regularly to newspapers and magazines and is the author of 16 books.

Daniel Schacter (1952–)

Best known for his work on human memory, Daniel Schacter was born in New York. His PhD thesis at the University of Toronto was supervised by Endel Tulving, and in 1981 the pair set up a unit for memory disorders at Toronto. Ten years later, Schacter became a professor of psychology at Harvard, where he established the Schacter Memory Laboratory.

Martin Seligman (1942–)

Martin Seligman is regarded as one of the founding fathers of positive psychology. Born in New York, he studied philosophy at Princeton University, and earned his PhD in psychology at the University of Pennsylvania. Inspired by the work of Aaron Beck, Seligman developed an interest in depression and the search for happiness. He is the director of the Penn Positive Psychology Center, and was elected president of the American Psychological Association for 1998.

B. F. Skinner (1904–1990)

Born in Pennsylvania, Burrhus Frederic Skinner studied English at Hamilton College in Clinton, New York, and initially wanted to be a writer. Influenced by the work of Ivan Pavlov and John B. Watson, he earned his doctorate in psychology at Harvard and became a pioneer of behaviorism. He received a lifetime achievement award from the American Psychological Association a few days before he died.

Thomas Szasz (1920–2012)

Thomas Szasz, author of *The Myth of Mental Illness*, was a well-known critic of the moral and scientific foundations of psychiatry. Born in Budapest, Hungary, he moved to the United States in 1938 and studied medicine at the University of Cincinnati. He later taught at New York State University, and was honored with more than 50 prestigious awards.

Edward Thorndike (1874–1949)

Born in Massachusetts, Edward Thorndike is known for his work on animal behavior and the learning process. He studied at Harvard under William James and completed his doctoral thesis at Columbia University, where he spent nearly his entire career. He helped lay the scientific foundations for modern educational psychology, and was the president of the American Psychological Society for 1912.

Edward Tolman (1886–1959)

Edward Tolman was a behaviorist who is known for his experiments with rats in mazes. He studied electrochemistry at the Massachusetts Institute of Technology, but, after reading works by William James, opted for a graduate degree in psychology at Harvard. He taught at the University of California, Berkeley, for most of his life and made significant contributions to the studies of learning and motivation. He was the president of the American Psychological Society for 1937.

Endel Tulving (1927–)

Born the son of a judge in Estonia, Endel Tulving is an experimental psychologist and neuroscientist. He received his bachelor's and master's degrees from the University of Toronto, and his doctorate from Harvard, before returning to Toronto as a professor. He is recognized for his theories on the organization of memory and in 2005 won a Gairdner Foundation International Award—Canada's leading prize in biology and medicine.

Lev Vygotsky (1896–1934)

Lev Vygotsky was born in the town of Orsha in the Russian Empire (present-day Belarus). He studied law at Moscow State University, where he was influenced by Gestalt psychology. He is best known as a developmental psychologist for his theory that children learn through their social environment. Though not widely recognized during his lifetime, his work has become the basis of much research and theory in the field of cognitive development.

John B. Watson (1878–1958)

John Broadus Watson, founder of the school of behaviorism, was born into a poor family in South Carolina. Although he was a rebellious teenager, he left college with a master's degree at the age of 21. After earning his PhD at the University of Chicago, he became chair of the psychology department at Johns Hopkins University. He is known for his research on animal behavior and child rearing, as well as for his controversial Little Albert experiment. In 1915, he was the president of the American Psychological Society.

Max Wertheimer (1880–1943)

One of the founders of Gestalt psychology, Max Wertheimer was born in Prague into a well-educated family. A talented violinist and composer, he seemed destined to become a musician, but studied law, philosophy, and then psychology. He taught at universities in Berlin and Frankfurt, Germany, before emigrating to New York City in 1933. Wertheimer is best known for his work on how the mind looks for patterns when processing visual information.

Robert Zajonc (1923–2008)

Robert Zajonc was a Polish social psychologist known for his work on judgment and decision-making. When he was 16, his family fled from Łódź to Warsaw to escape the Nazi invasion. His parents were killed in an air raid and he was sent to a German labor camp, from which he escaped. He earned his bachelor's, master's, and doctoral degrees at the University of Michigan, and worked as a professor there for nearly four decades.

Bluma Zeigarnik (1901–1988)

Bluma Zeigarnik was born in Lithuania, then part of the Russian Empire, and was one of the first women in Russia to attend college. She earned her PhD at the University of Berlin, where she was influenced by Gestalt psychologists Wolfgang Köhler, Max Wertheimer, and Kurt Lewin. She received the Lewin Memorial Award in 1983 and is noted for her work on the tendency of people to remember incomplete tasks.

Philip Zimbardo (1933–)

Born in New York to a family of Sicilian immigrants, Philip Zimbardo attended Brooklyn College, where he completed a bachelor's degree in psychology, sociology, and anthropology. He earned his PhD from Yale, and taught at several universities before moving to Stanford University, where he created the famous Stanford prison experiment. He has authored many books, received numerous awards, and was elected president of the American Psychological Association for 2002.

Glossary

Aggression
Behavior that causes harm to another individual.

Altruism
The unselfish concern for the well-being of other people.

Attachment
An important emotional bond between a child and an adult caregiver, formed in the early years of the child's life.

Attention
The process of focusing our *perception* on one element in our environment.

Attitudes
The evaluations people make about objects, ideas, events, or other people.

Behaviorism
A psychological approach that studies observable behavior, rather than internal processes such as thinking or emotion.

Bystander effect
A phenomenon in which the more people who are present, the less likely one of them is to help a person in distress.

Classical conditioning
A type of learning in which a *stimulus* provokes an involuntary or automatic *response*.

Cognitive behavioral therapy (CBT)
A type of talk therapy that encourages patients to manage their problems by changing the way that they think and behave.

Cognitive bias
An illogical assumption that influences decision-making, often leading to bad judgments.

Cognitive dissonance
A feeling of unease that arises when someone holds two conflicting beliefs.

Cognitive psychology
The psychological approach that focuses on mental processes, including learning, memory, *perception*, and *attention*.

Computerized tomography (CT) scanning
A type of brain-scanning technology that uses X-rays and a computer to create detailed images of the inside of the body.

Collective unconscious
In Carl Jung's theory, the part of the *unconscious* that is shared with other people, and is passed on from generation to generation.

Conditioned response
In *classical conditioning*, a *response* that is learned or becomes associated with a specific *stimulus*.

Conformity
The tendency for people to adopt the behaviors, *attitudes*, and values of other members of a group or an authority figure.

Consciousness
The awareness people have of themselves and their environment.

Context-dependent memory
A memory that is associated with the place where it was recorded, and can be recalled when a person revisits that place.

Control group
A group of participants in a study who are not exposed to the conditions of that experiment.

Crystallized intelligence
The ability to use knowledge and skills acquired through education and experience.

Dependence
The inability to stop using a substance such as alcohol.

Depression
A mood disorder characterized by feelings of hopelessness and low self-esteem.

Drive
A trigger that motivates people to satisfy physiological needs. For example, the drive of hunger encourages people to eat.

Ego
In *psychoanalysis*, the conscious and rational part of the mind.

Electroconvulsive therapy (ECT)
A treatment for mental disorders, in which an electric current is passed through the brain to induce a fit.

Electroencephalography (EEG)
A type of brain-scanning technology that measures electrical signals in the brain.

Epilepsy
A disorder marked by sudden seizures, associated with abnormal electrical activity in the brain.

Episodic memory
The memory store that records events and experiences.

Extrovert
A personality type that directs its energy toward the outside world. Extroverts are often outgoing and talkative, and enjoy the company of other people.

False memory
A recovered memory of an event that did not take place.

Flashbulb memory
A vivid memory associated with an emotional event.

Flow
Mihály Csíkszentmihályi's term for the trancelike state people enter when they are totally absorbed in a task, leading to feelings of satisfaction and happiness.

Fluid intelligence
The capacity to solve problems through reasoning, independent of acquired knowledge.

Free association
A technique used in *psychotherapy*, in which patients say the first thing that comes to mind after any given word—used to reveal their *unconscious* thoughts.

Freudian slip
An act or word that is close to but different from the one intended, and reflects *unconscious* thoughts.

Frontal lobe
One of the four areas or lobes of the brain. Located at the front of each *hemisphere*, it is associated with *short-term memory*.

Functional magnetic resonance imaging (fMRI)
A type of brain-scanning technology that measures blood flow to areas of the brain.

General intelligence
An ability that underlies all intelligent behavior, proposed by Charles Spearman.

Gestalt psychology
A psychological approach that emphasizes the "whole" above its individual parts, in mental processes such as perception.

Gestalt therapy
A form of *psychotherapy* that focuses on an individual's present experiences, and emphasizes personal responsibility.

Groupthink
A phenomenon that occurs in a group of people when the desire to conform overrides independent critical thinking, often leading to bad decision-making.

Hemisphere
Either of the halves of the brain. Human brains are divided into the left and right hemispheres.

Hypnosis
The induction of a temporary, trancelike state of *consciousness*, in which a person is more susceptible to suggestions.

Hypothesis
A prediction or statement tested by experimentation.

Id
In *psychoanalysis*, the *unconsious* part of the mind that is associated with our instinctive *drives* and physical needs.

Imprinting
An instinctive phenomenon in which a newborn animal will bond with any individual or object it identifies as its parent.

Inferiority complex
A condition that develops when a person feels inferior to other people. It can lead to hostile or antisocial behavior.

In-group
A group to which one belongs. Members will often view their group more favorably than other groups, or *out-groups*.

Innate
When a characteristic is present from birth, rather than acquired through experience. It may or may not be inherited.

Intelligence quotient (IQ)
A numerical representation of a person's intelligence, which shows how much more or less intelligent he or she is than the average, an IQ of 100.

Introspection
The examination of one's own inner state and thoughts.

Introvert
A personality type that directs its energy toward itself. Introverts are often shy and quiet.

Long-term memory
The memory store that holds information for a long time.

Mind
The element of a person that controls *consciousness* and thought.

Modeling
A type of learning in which individuals decide how to act by observing the behavior of others.

Mood-dependent memory
A memory that is related to a particular mood, and is recalled when a person feels that way again.

Morality
The set of *values* and beliefs held by a community about what is right and wrong.

Nervous system
The body's control center, consisting of the brain, spinal cord, and nerves.

Neurodegenerative disease
A disease that impairs the *nervous system*.

Neuron
A nerve cell that carries signals to and from all parts of the body, and forms networks in the brain.

Neuroplasticity
The way that the connections in the brain adapt to changes in an individual's behavior or environment, or change as a result of brain injury.

Neuroscience
The biological study of the brain and how it works.

Neurosis
A mental disorder that has no apparent physical cause, such as anxiety or *depression*.

Non-rapid-eye-movement (NREM) sleep
A stage of sleep when the muscles relax and brain activity, breathing, and heart rate slow down.

Operant conditioning
A type of learning in which a voluntary *response* is reinforced by a reward or punishment.

Out-group
A group to which one does not belong, and may, therefore, be viewed unfavorably.

Perception
The way that people organize, identify, and interpret information from the *senses* in order to understand their environment.

Personality
A person's unique combination of *traits* or characteristics that incline him or her to behave and think in a certain way.

Phobia
An anxiety disorder characterized by an intense, irrational fear of an object or situation.

Prejudice
Preconceived, usually unfavorable judgments toward people because of gender, social class, age, religion, race, or other personal characteristics.

Procedural memory
The memory store that records methods and how to do things.

Psychiatry
The medical field dedicated to the study, diagnosis, and treatment of mental disorders.

Psychoactive drugs
Substances that affect our *consciousness* by changing the way signals are passed around our brains and *nervous systems*.

Psychoanalysis
The theories and therapeutic methods, developed by Sigmund Freud, that aim to treat mental disorders by unlocking *unconscious* thoughts.

Psychopathy
A personality disorder, characterized by a distinct lack of empathy or remorse, and antisocial behavior.

Psychotherapy
Therapeutic treatments that use psychological rather than medical means.

Rapid-eye-movement (REM) sleep
The stage of sleep when we dream, characterized by rapid movements of the eyes and immobilization of the muscles.

Reinforcement
In *classical conditioning*, the procedure that increases the likelihood of a *response*.

Repression
A defense mechanism in which painful thoughts, feelings, or memories are excluded from conscious thought.

Response
A reaction to an object, event, or situation.

Schizophrenia
A severe mental disorder characterized by a distorted vision of reality, with symptoms including hallucinations, erratic behavior, and lack of emotion.

Self-actualization
The human need to achieve one's unique, full potential—one of the most advanced human needs, according to Abraham Maslow.

Self-transcendence
The human need to do things for a higher cause than oneself.

Semantic memory
The memory store that records facts and knowledge.

Senses
The faculties we use to perceive changes in our internal and external environments. The five senses are hearing, smell, sight, taste, and touch.

Short-term memory
The memory store that holds information that people need for doing things now. The information will be lost if it is not moved into *long-term memory*.

Social learning
Albert Bandura's theory of learning based on individuals observing and copying (*modeling*) the behavior of others.

Social loafing
The phenomenon in which people deliberately exert less effort to achieve a goal when they work in a group than when they work alone.

Social norms
The unwritten rules that govern the behavior or *attitudes* of a community.

Split brain
The result when the two *hemispheres* of the brain are surgically separated, originally used to treat *epilepsy*.

Stimulus
Any object, event, situation, or factor in an environment that triggers a specific *response*.

Superego
In *psychoanalysis*, the term for our inner "conscience," or what we have been told is right and wrong.

Synesthesia
A condition in which sufferers perceive letters, numbers, or days of the week as having different colors, or even personalities.

Synaptic transmission
The process of communicating information between *neurons*, in which one neuron fires a signal at a neighboring neuron.

Trait
A specific personal characteristic that occurs consistently and influences behavior across a range of situations.

Unconditioned response
In *classical conditioning*, a reflexive or natural *response* elicited in reaction to a particular *stimulus*.

Unconscious
According to Sigmund Freud, the level of *consciousness* that cannot be accessed easily and stores our deepest ideas, desires, memories, and emotions.

Values
A set of principles, standards of behavior, or things people judge to be important in life.

Index

Note: Bold page numbers are used to indicate key information on the topic.

A

abnormal behavior 104–107
academic psychologists 8–9
addiction 53, **100–101**, 117
Adler, Alfred 111
advertisements 117, **130–131**, 147
aggression 132–133
Ainsworth, Mary 14–15, **30–31**
Allport, Gordon 86, **88–89**, 96, 140
altruism **124–125**, 134–135
Ames, Adelbert, Jr. 78
amputation 48
anger 132–133
animal behavior 14, 15, 18–19, 22, 26, 58, 140
antidepressants 112, 116
antipsychiatry movement 107
antisocial personality disorder (APD) 108–109
applause, crowd 121
applied psychologists **8–9**, 71
Aronson, Elliot 75, 107
Asch, Solomon 120–121, **126–127**
assemblies (brain) 40
asylums 112
attachment **14–15**, 31, 144
attention **68–69**, 70
attitudes 128–129
attraction 145

audience effect 140–141, 147
authority figures 28–29, 122–123, 134, 135, 138–139
aversion therapy 113

B

babies 14–15, 30, 34, 35, 77, 143
see also childhood
bad behavior 108–109, 122–123
Baddeley, Alan 61
Bandura, Albert 26, 27, 28, 72, 132, 142
Baron-Cohen, Simon 143
Bartlett, Frederic 65
Batson, Daniel 124, 125
Beauvoir, Simone de 142
Beck, Aaron 98, 99, 113
behavior 6–7, **26–27**
abnormal 104–107
animal 14, 15, 18–19, 22, 26, 58, 140
antisocial 35
good and bad 28–29, 108–109, 122–125, 134–135
motives and drives 89, 94
researching 11
behavior therapy 113
behaviorists **18–19**, 20, 26, 28, 58, 72, 85, 94, 130
beliefs **74–75**, 129
Bentall, Richard 107
Berkowitz, Leonard 133
Bettelheim, Bruno 15
Binet, Alfred 90
biological psychology 8, 39, **52–53**, 85
Blakemore, Colin 41
blood-brain barrier 53

body clock 50, **51**, 52
Bower, Gordon H 61
Bowlby, John 14, 144
brain 36–53
areas of 43
consciousness states 47
damage 32, 39, **42–43**, 53, 105
development 34
electroconvulsive therapy 112
and language 72–73
left and right hemispheres 43
male and female 143
neurons **40–41**, 44, 52, 53
pattern perception 76–77
scans 39, 41, 42
size 91
surgery 112
visual processing 48
brainwashing 131
Breuer, Josef 102, 110
Broadbent, Donald 68, 69, **70–71**
Broca, Paul 42, 72
Brown, James A. C. 131
Brown, Roger 61
Bruner, Jerome 21, 25, 57, 78
bullying 146
bystander effect **124–125**, 146

C

camouflage 81
Candid Camera 126
Capgras delusion 49
career choice 117
Cattell, Raymond 86, 91

character see personality
Charcot, Jean-Martin 102, 110
Cherry, Colin 68–69
childhood 14–17, 30–31, 34–35, 52, 91, 132
and language 73
moral development 28–29
Chomsky, Noam 72–73
Clark, Kenneth and Mamie 27
cockroaches 140
cognitive behavioral therapy (CBT) **113**, 131
cognitive biases 59
cognitive dissonance 74–75
cognitive psychology 8, 61, **80–81**, 113
collective unconscious 111
competition 140–141
conditioning
classical **18–19**, 22–23, 26, 28
operant 26–27
as therapy 113
conformity **120–123**, 126, 128–129, 136, 147
conscience 108, 110
consciousness **46–47**, 50, 110
Crick, Francis 47
crime 108–109, 124
criminal profiling 108
crowds 121, 125
Csíkszentmihályi, Mihály 115

D

Darley, John M. 124–125
Darwin, Charles 84, 85, 92
decision-making 34, **58–59**, 125

depression 98–99
Descartes, René 38
desensitization 113
developmental psychology
  9, 16–17, 21, 28–29,
  34–35, 72, 142
difference, psychology of
  116–117
dogs, Pavlov's 18–19, 22
Dollard, John 132–133
dreams **50–51**, 61
  interpretation of 103, 111
drives 89, 94
drugs
  addiction to 53, **100–101**
  effect on brain 40
  therapeutic 112

E

Eagly, Alice 142
Ebbinghaus, Hermann
  20–21, 57, 60
education *see* learning
ego 110
Einstein, Albert 91
Ekman, Paul 92–93
electric shock experiments
  122–123, 132, 134
electroconvulsive therapy
  (ECT) 112
Ellis, Albert 98–99, 113
embarrassment 75
emotional stability 86, 87
emotions 92–93
  detecting 99
empathy **124**, 125, 143
endorphins 116
Erikson, Erik 17, 32
essence 76
evil **108–109**, 122–123

evolution 85, 132
exercise 25, 116
  in old age 33
experts 131
extroversion 86, 87
eyewitness accounts 62,
  63, 81
Eysenck, Hans **86–87**,
  96, 111

F

facial expressions 93, 116
fathers 15, 31
fear 130, 131
feminism 142
Festinger, Leon 74–75
fight-or-flight response 51
first impressions 87
flashbulb memories 60,
  61
flow 115
Fodor, Jerry 38
Foster, Russell 50
Franklin, George 62
free association 103
Freud, Anna 110
Freud, Sigmund 47, 50, 94,
  102–103, 110–111, 112,
  114, 132
Freudian slip 111
friendship 144, 146
Frijda, Nico 92
Fromm, Erich 114
frustration 132–133

G

Gage, Phineas 42
Galton, Francis 85

Gardner, Howard 91
gender 73, 93, **142–143**
genetics 84–85
Gesell, Arnold 85
Gestalt psychology **76–77**,
  78, 126, 136
Gestalt therapy 111
Gibson, J. J. 79
Golgi, Camillo 40
good behavior 28–29,
  124–125, 134–135
good life 114–115
Good Samaritan
  experiment 125
Goodman, Paul 111
grammar 73
groups **120–121**, 124–125,
  128–129, 131, **136–139**
groupthink 136–137
Guilford, J P 91
Guthrie, Edwin 19

H

habits, bad 117
handshakes 147
happiness 107, **114–115**
Hare, Robert D. 108–109
Harlow, Harry 15
Hebb, Donald 40
hedonism 94
helping behavior 124–125,
  134–135
Hitler, Adolf 103, 131
HM (case study) 42
hobbies 95
home life 35
Hull, Clark 94
hypnosis 45, 62, **102**,
  110
"hysteria" 110

I

id 110
impression-forming 126,
  127
imprinting 14
indoctrination 131
inferiority complex 111
information processing
  68–69, 71
insanity 106–107
intelligence 90–91
  multiple types of 117
interviews 10
introspection 46, 47
introversion 86, 87
investigative psychology 108
IQ (intelligence quotient)
  90–91

J

James, William 46–47, 93
Janis, Irving 136–137
Jenness, A. 120
Jung, Carl 111

K

Kahneman, Daniel 58–59
karate 33
Kastenbaum, Robert 33
Katz, Daniel 128
Kelly, George 87
kindness, acts of 115
knowledge 56–57
  see also learning
Kohlberg, Lawrence 28–29
Köhler, Wolfgang 21, 58, 76
Kraepelin, Emil 105

L

laboratory conditions 10–11
Laing, R. D. 107
Lange, Carl 93
language 34, 42, 43, **72–73**, 127, 131
Lashley, Karl 42–43
Latané, Bibb 124–125, 141
Lazarus, Richard 93
leadership 137, **138–139**
learning **20–21, 24–25**, 56–57
  gender and 143
  hands-on 21, 34
  in old age 33
  social 27
  see also memory
Lewin, Kurt 136, 138
Little Albert 19
Loftus, Elizabeth **62–63**, 67
Lorenz, Konrad 14, 132
love 144–145
lying 28, 116

M

Maccoby, Eleanor E. 143
madness *see* insanity
magnetic fields 52
management style 138–139
Maslow, Abraham 95, 96, 114
maturation 85
May, Rollo 99
Mayo, Elton 138, 139
McGregor, Douglas 139
medical psychologists 8–9
memory 20–21, **60–61**
  early 35
  false 62, 63, 67

long-term 42, 61, 64
  old age and 32–33
  poor recall 66–67
  repressed 110
  short-term 64, 69
  storing 64–65, 66
  techniques 81
  types of 64, 65
  unwanted 67
men 93, **142–143**
Mendel, Gregor 84, 85
mental disorders 104–107
  therapies 112–113
mental health 114
metaphors 127
movies 35, 132
Milgram, Stanley 122–123, **134–135**
Miller, George Armitage 69
Miller, Neal E. 132
Mills, Judson 75
mimicry 34, 53, 132
mind 38–39
  see also brain
Mischel, Walter 97
moods 61, **92–93**
morality 28–29
mothers 14–15, 30–31
motivation 89, **94–95**
multitasking 69, 80
music 115

N

nature versus nurture debate 84–85
Nazis 103, 122, 131
needs, hierarchy of 95
negative reinforcement 26–27
negativity 17, 113, 128

neural pathways 40–41
neurodegenerative diseases 32
neurons **40–41**, 44, 52
  mirror 53
neuroplasticity 41
neuroscience **38–39**, 41, 42, 44–45, 47, 48–49, 112
neurosis 110, 112
neuroticism 86, 87
normality 104–105
norms, social 27, 29, 128–129

O

obedience **122–123**, 134, 136
old age **32–33**, 144
open-mindedness 116
opinions 126, 128–129, 130–131
optical illusions 78–79

P

parents **14–15**, 25, 35, 52, 72
  see also fathers; mothers
patterns 76–77
Pavlov, Ivan 18–19, **22–23**
perception 76–79
Perls, Fritz and Laura 111
personality 84–89
  changes in 96–97
  disorders 108–109
  tests 117
  type theory versus trait theory 86, 96, 97
perspective 77, 79
persuasion 130–131
phantom limbs 48

phobias 113
phrenology 38
Piaget, Jean 16–17, 21, 24–25, 28, 57, 72
Pinker, Steven 73
play 21, 24, 28, 94
politics 128, 131, 146
positive psychology 114–115
positive reinforcement 26–27
positivity 17, 114, 128
post-traumatic stress disorder (PTSD) 67, 112–113
prejudice 27, 129
prison experiment 123
problem-solving 58
propaganda 126, 131
psychiatry **104–105**, 106, 112
psychoanalysis 102–103, **110–111**, 112–113, 114
psychologists, types of 8–9
psychology explained 6–7
psychopaths 108–109
psychotherapy **112–113**, 114
psychoticism 86
punishment 22, 26–27, 28

Q

questionnaires 10

R

racism 27, 129
Ramachandran, Vilayanur 48–49
Ramón y Cajal, Santiago 40, **44–45**

Rational Emotive Behavior Therapy 113
reading 80
reasoning 58–59
reinforcement
  accidental 34
  positive and negative 26–27
relationships 144–145
religious cults 131
repression 110
research methods 10–11
Revonsuo, Antti 51
reward 26–27, 28, 94
rhyming 81
right and wrong 28–29
Rogers, Carl 96, 114
Rowe, Dorothy 99
rules 29
Rutter, Michael 15

S
sadness 98–99
scans 39, 42
scapegoat 132
Schacter, Daniel 66
schema 65
schizophrenia 105, 106–107
seasonal affective disorder (SAD) 116
self-actualization 95
self-awareness 17
self-destruction 132
selfishness 124–125, 132
Seligman, Martin 99, 114–115
senses 76–77
Shepard, Roger 78
Sherif, Muzafer 137
Siffre, Michel 51

Simon, Théodore 90
situationism 97
Skinner, B. F. 20, 26–27, 56, 72, 94
sleep **50–51**, 52, 59
sleepwalking 53
smoking 74, 117, 120, 131
social learning theory 27
social loafing 141
social networking 146
social norms 27, 29, 128–129
social psychology 85, **120–123**, 128–129
Spearman, Charles 91
Sperry, Roger 43
sports 95, 106, 128, **140–141**
stage fright 147
Stanford prison experiment 123
statistics 11
Sternberg, Robert 91, 144–145
Strange Situation experiment **14–15**, 31
stream of consciousness 46–47
strokes 32
superfoods 65
superstition 34
synapses 40
synaptic transmission 40–41
synesthesia 49
Szasz, Thomas 101, 105, 107

T
talking cure 103, **110**, 111
team spirit 136–139, 141
teenagers 50, 52
television 27, 135

Thatcher, Margaret 142
therapy 112–113
Thorndike, Edward 19, 20, 26, 32–33, 56
three-dimensional perception 77
Three Faces of Eve, The 97
Tolman, Edward 21, 58
Tononi, Giulio 46, 47
trait theory 86, 96, 97
trepanning 113
Triplett, Norman 140
Tulving, Endel 61, 64–65
Tversky, Amos 58–59
twins, identical 85
type theory 86, 96, 97

U
unconscious, the 47, 50, **102–103**, 110–111
unknown, fear of 130

V
values 89
video games 35, 132
violence 132–133
  in movies and games 35, 132
vision 48, 77, 78–79
Vygotsky, Lev 25, 57

W
Watson, John B. **18–19**, 26, 56, 85, **130–131**
Weisberg, Deena 39
Wernicke, Carl 42, 72

Wertheimer, Max 76, 126
Whyte, William H. 136
Wolpe, Joseph 112–113
women 93, **142–143**
working conditions 71
World War II 122, 126
Wundt, William 46

Y
yawning 50

Z
Zajonc, Robert 93, 130, 140–141, 144
Zeigarnik, Bluma 61
Zimbardo, Philip 123, 124, 135

Acknowledgments

The publisher would like to thank Jeongeun Yule Park for design assistance, John Searcy for proofreading, and Jackie Brind for the index.

The publisher would like to thank the following for their kind permission to reproduce their photographs:

(Key: a–above; b–below/bottom; c–center; f–far; l–left; r–right; t–top)

6 Dorling Kindersley: Whipple Museum of History of Science, Cambridge (cr). **Getty Images:** Pasieka / Science Photo Library (cl); Smith Collection / Stone (c). **7 Getty Images:** Rich Legg / E+ (cr). Pearson Asset Library: Pearson Education Ltd / Studio 8 (cla). **12 Corbis:** Matthieu Spohn / PhotoAlto. **15 Science Photo Library:** Science Source (br). **17 Pearson Asset Library:** Pearson Education Ltd / Tudor Photography (tr). **29 Pearson Asset Library:** Pearson Education Asia Ltd / Terry Leung (br/doll). **30-31 Dorling Kindersley:** Dr. Patricia Crittenden (portrait). **36-37 Getty Images:** Laurence Mouton / PhotoAlto. **39 PunchStock:** Image Source (br). **42 Bright Bytes Studio:** photograph of daguerreotype by Jack Wilgus (bc). **44-45 Dorling Kindersley:** Science Photo Library (portrait). **48-49 Dorling Kindersley:** Rex Features / Charles Sykes (portrait). **54 Corbis:** momentimages / Tetra Images. **62-63 Dorling Kindersley:** Courtesy of UC Irvine (portrait). **69 Corbis:** Martin Palombini / Moodboard (br/gorilla). **70 Dorling Kindersley:** Science Photo Library / Corbin O'Grady Studio (portrait). **72 Pearson Asset Library:** Pearson Education Asia Ltd / Coleman Yuen (bc). **75 Dreamstime.com:** Horiyan (br/table). **78 Corbis:** Peter Endig / DPA (bl). **82 Getty Images:** Robbert Koene / Gallo Images. **85 Getty Images:** Image Source (br). **87 Pearson Asset Library:** Pearson Education Asia Ltd / Coleman Yuen (br). **88-89 Dorling Kindersley:** Corbis / Bettmann (portrait). **93 Corbis:** John Woodworth / Loop Images (br). **97 Corbis:** John Springer Collection (br). **107 Pearson Asset Library:** Pearson Education Ltd / Jon Barlow (br). **111 Pearson Asset Library:** Pearson Education Ltd / Jörg Carstensen (br). **115 Pearson Asset Library:** Pearson Education Ltd / Lord and Leverett (br). **118-119 Corbis:** Stretch Photography / Blend Images. **121 Corbis:** Chat Roberts (tr). **125 Pearson Asset Library:** Pearson Education Ltd / Tudor Photography (br). **126-127 Dorling Kindersley:** Solomon Asch Center for Study of Ethnopolitical Conflict. **129 Corbis:** John Collier Jr. (br). **132 Dreamstime.com:** Horiyan (bc/table). **134-135 Dorling Kindersley:** Manuscripts and Archives, Yale University Library / Courtesy of Alexandra Milgram (portrait). **137 Corbis:** Geon-soo Park / Sung-Il Kim (br). **143 Corbis:** Adrian Samson (br). **144 Corbis:** Hannes Hepp (bc).

All other images © Dorling Kindersley
For further information see: www.dkimages.com